PELICAN BOOK A666

SHAKESPEARE: A CELEBRATION
1564–1964

EDITED BY T. J. B. SPENCER

T. J. B. Spencer was born in 1915 and educated at
the Lower School of John Lyon, Harrow. He
graduated at the University of London and served
from 1941 to 1946 in the Army during the Second
World War. After holding appointments at King's
College, and University College, London, he
became Professor of English at the Queen's
University of Belfast (1955–8). He was then
appointed Professor of English Language and
Literature at the University of Birmingham, and in
addition Director of the Shakespeare Institute in 1961.

Professor Spencer is the author of *Fair Greece, Sad
Relic* (a study of English philhellenism from
Shakespeare to Byron), *The Tyranny of Shakespeare*
(the British Academy Shakespeare lecture, 1959),
Byron and the Greek Tradition, *From Gibbon to
Darwin*, *Shakespeare: The Roman Plays*, and other
contributions to scholarship and criticism. He is
general editor of the *Modern Language Review*, the
quarterly journal of the Modern Humanities
Research Association. For Penguins he has recently
edited *Shakespeare's Plutarch* (the four lives in
Sir Thomas North's translation which were used by
Shakespeare in the composition of his Roman plays).

*The frontispiece shows part of John Speed's map
of Warwickshire, 1610*

HEMLING [D] HUNDRED

Escote
Solihull
Hampton in Arden
Alesley
THE

Henwood
Barston
Barkswell
Fletchamsted
COVENT

Langdon Hall
Ridfen
Stichall

Knoll
Bale Hall
Quenes park
The Chase
Kenelworth

T OF
Packwood
Hunsiyley
Stonley

ON HUND.
Baddesley Clinton
Goodrest Lodge
Ashow
Ston

Larproth
Kingswood
Roxhall
Lekewotton
Weston und wethel

Brome
Haseley
Wedgenok park
Woodlowe
Milverton
Edmondscote
Lilling

Preston Bagot
Rowinton
Hatton
Budbrook
Guy Cliff
Lemington Hastings

Clayerdon
Pinley Grove
Hampton Ourley
WARWICK
Radford Semel
Whit

Henley in Ardē
Langley
Woluerding ton
Norton Limsey
Avon flu

E HUNDRED
Edson
Sherborne
Barford
Tachbroo

Bearley
Snitterfeld
Wasperton
Newbolde
Wellesborn
Ashborne

Aston Cantlow
Bishopton
Clopton
Charlcot
Morton Morell

Bilsley
Bishops Hampto
Leightho
Bisf

Stretford upon Auen
Aulston
Loxley
Walton
Compton Mardock

Draiton
Bridgton
King Gaidon

Luddington
Clifford
Goldscots park
Combroke
Kyneton
Chads

Milcote
Atherston
PART OF
WORCES:
Kyneton H

Welford
Preston
Butlers Marston
Over Eatnton

Whitchuch
Alder Aarston
Nether Eatnton
Nether Pillerton
KYNETON H
Burton

Shakespeare:
A Celebration

1564–1964

EDITED BY
T. J. B. SPENCER

PENGUIN BOOKS

BALTIMORE · MARYLAND

Penguin Books Ltd, Harmondsworth, Middlesex, England
Penguin Books Inc., 3300 Clipper Mill Road,
Baltimore 11, Md, U.S.A.
Penguin Books Pty Ltd, Ringwood, Victoria, Australia

First published 1964

Made and printed in Great Britain
by Hazell Watson & Viney Ltd
Aylesbury, Bucks
Set in Linotype Granjon

CONTENTS

PR
2899
S7

LIST OF PLATES

b Harvard House, Stratford-upon-Avon, home of
Katherine Rogers, mother of John Harvard,
the founder of Harvard College.
(*Edwin Smith*.)

9a Shakespeare's monument in Holy Trinity
Church. (*Edwin Smith*.)
b Shakespeare's gravestone. (*Edwin Smith*.)

10 The nave of Holy Trinity Church,
Stratford-upon-Avon. (*Edwin Smith*.)

11 The garden and site of New Place,
Shakespeare's last home, overlooking the
Guild Chapel. (*Edwin Smith*.)

12a Queen Elizabeth in her coronation robes;
an anonymous painting probably of 1559
(Warwick Castle). (*Courtauld Institute
of Art*.)
b Henry Wriothesley, third Earl of
Southampton. Portrait by an unknown artist
about 1601–3, when Southampton was
imprisoned in the Tower of London.
(*Welbeck Abbey*.)

13 Bankside, from Visscher's *View of London*,
1616. (*Thames and Hudson, Ltd*.)

14 Martin Droeshout's engraving of Shakespeare.
The earliest known state; from a copy
of the First Folio. (*Folger Shakespeare Library,
Washington, D.C.*)

15 The first draft of Sir William Dethick's entries
in the Heralds' College as to the
assignment of arms to John Shakespeare,
1596–9.

16a Richard Burbage: perhaps a self-portrait
(a detail from the picture in the
Dulwich Gallery.) (*The College Governors
of Alleyn's College of God's Gift, Dulwich*.)
b Thomas Betterton: a painting by (or after)
Sir Godfrey Kneller. (*National Portrait Gallery*.)

17 David Garrick and Mrs Pritchard in *Macbeth*:
watercolour by Henry Fuseli about 1766.
(*Kunsthaus, Zürich*.)

18a Sarah Siddons as Lady Macbeth sleep-walking; by G. H. Harlow. (*Garrick Club, London.*)

b John Philip Kemble as Coriolanus, by Sir Thomas Lawrence, 1798. (*Guildhall Art Gallery, London.*)

19a Edmund Kean as Richard III, by J. J. Halls, 1815. (*Victoria and Albert Museum, London.*)

b Sir Henry Irving as King Lear, by Bernard Partridge: from the Souvenir Programme, Lyceum Theatre, London, 1892.

20a Ellen Terry as Portia in *The Merchant of Venice*: from *The Illustrated London News*, 1880.

b The Souvenir Programme of Sir Beerbohm Tree's production of *Twelfth Night*, 1902.

21 Sir Laurence Olivier as Malvolio in *Twelfth Night*, Stratford-upon-Avon, 1955. (*The Royal Shakespeare Theatre, Stratford-upon-Avon. Photograph Angus McBean.*)

22a Paul Scofield as King Lear and Alan Webb as Gloucester, Stratford-upon-Avon, 1962. (*The Royal Shakespeare Theatre, Stratford-upon-Avon. Photograph Gordon Goode.*)

b Sir Laurence Olivier as Richard III, and Sir Ralph Richardson as Richmond, the Old Vic, 1944-5. (*John Vickers.*)

23a A scene from Sir Tyrone Guthrie's production of *All's Well That Ends Well*, Stratford-upon-Avon, 1959. (*The Royal Shakespeare Theatre, Stratford-upon-Avon. Photograph T. F. Holte.*)

b A scene from the National Youth Theatre's production of *Hamlet*, Sarah Bernhardt Theatre, Paris, 1960. (*Photo Pic, Paris.*)

24a Peter O'Toole as Shylock, Stratford-upon-Avon, 1960. (*The Royal Shakespeare Theatre, Stratford-upon-Avon. Photograph T. F. Holte.*)

b Vanessa Redgrave as Rosalind in *As You Like It*, Stratford-upon-Avon, 1961. (*The Royal Shakespeare Theatre, Stratford-upon-Avon. Photograph T. F. Holte.*)

LIST OF TEXT FIGURES

FOREWORD

No writer in the world holds a position similar to Shakespeare's. There are other great poets of international status (Homer, Dante); there are other great English writers who are widely translated (Bunyan, Dickens). But the living reputation of these writers cannot seriously compare with that of Shakespeare, whose plays are being performed more often and in more countries of the world than ever before. And even those people who do not read his plays, nor see them performed on the stage, have become familiar with some of his more popular works in the cinema and on the television screen. As Mr John Russell Taylor reminds us (p. 103 below), probably more human beings saw the Royal Shakespeare Company's production of *As You Like It* on television than had seen it during the whole of its previous history on the stage, from Shakespeare's time to the present day.

Shakespeare is the subject of this *Celebration* because his plays provide delight and exhilaration and profound tragic experience to audiences in every country of the world. A combination of exquisite poetic sensitivity, a close observation of human character, and an incomparable mastery of language, enabled him to be a creator of imaginative visions of pathos and mirth which (whether read in the book or witnessed in the theatre) fill the mind and linger there.

But this is not a book of 'appreciation' of Shakespeare, nor merely of 'homage'. It does not try to explain the greatness of his poetry; nor to make a technical assessment of his stage-craft; nor to describe his impact upon the literature of other countries. It is intended for those who take the opportunity of the four-hundredth anniversary of Shakespeare's birth to consider the stages by which Shakespeare has achieved his commanding position in literature and in the theatre. It will, we hope, provide an agreeable and accurate companion for the visitor to Stratford-upon-Avon – or, for that matter, to the other Stratfords in Canada and the United States. Of the essays included here, Mr Laurence Kitchin's on the modern stage, and Mr John Russell Taylor's on film, sound broad-casting, and television, focus the attention on Shakespeare's position in entertainment at the present time. Dr J. R. Brown on the actors' interpretation of the plays and Professor Kenneth Muir on the editors and critics help to interpret the present by explaining the development from the past. Mr Norman Scarfe, Professor Charles J. Sisson, and the Editor try to make Shakespeare plain in his own world. The last essay in the book describes the ways by which, since Garrick's 'Jubilee' in Stratford-upon-Avon in 1769, homage has been paid to Shakespeare's genius, culminating in the extraordinary world-wide festivities of the Fourth Centenary in 1964.

We have to thank the officials of the Birmingham Museum and Art Gallery, of Shakespeare's Birthplace Trust, and of the Library and Art Gallery of the Royal Shakespeare Theatre, and our colleagues of the Barber Institute of Fine Arts, for their help, including the loan of photographs.

T. J. B. Spencer

The Shakespeare Institute,
    University of Birmingham

SHAKESPEARE:
STRATFORD-UPON-AVON
AND WARWICKSHIRE

Norman Scarfe

NE century after Shakespeare's birth, the monarchy and its consorts the church and the theatre were restored, and Sir Andrew Aguecheek could again fetch a laugh with his reaction to the news that there was a puritan streak in Malvolio:

O! if I thought that, I'd beat him like a dog!

Already the vicar of Stratford-upon-Avon was bothered by visitors, and reduced to writing in his diary: 'Remember to peruse Shakespeare's plays and be versed in them, that I may not be ignorant in that matter.' He collected what gossip he could, including the story of the first Shakespeare celebration, in 1616, the one that may have caused his death: 'Shakespeare, Drayton, and Ben Jonson had a merry meeting and it seems drank too hard, for Shakespeare died of a fever there contracted.'

Before a second century was up, the first season of Shakespeare's plays had run successfully in Stratford, and from a benefit performance of *Othello* the headmaster of the grammar-school had raised enough money to repair the poet's monument in the parish church. The owner of New Place, Shakespeare's large house and family seat from 1597, found himself in terrible trouble in 1756 for felling an old mulberry tree in the garden, a tree that Shakespeare *might have planted*. He was tired of people clamouring to see it. He went further and pulled down New Place itself (Plates 1 and 11). It had already, before 1702, been completely transformed from an Elizabethan gabled house to a formal sash-windowed and pedimented one. No matter; it was associated with Shakespeare; and the barbarous owner was banished the town! By the time Garrick had inaugurated the new Town Hall (Plate 1) in September 1769, with the effigy of Shakespeare as its principal feature, Shakespeare-worship was established, and Stratford became a centre of pilgrimage complete with holy places.

By 1785 London's influence was noticeable in Stratford. The Hon. John Byng was able to order dinner from a bill of fare equal to that of the Piazza Coffee House, Covent Garden. ('London prices' are among the first things observed at Stratford by the streams of American pilgrims today; but other metropolitan qualities are there, especially in the acting, cooking, and haberdashery.) Byng found Mrs Hart, the custodian of the birthplace, well provided with relics. He finally came away from Stratford highly pleased with a chunk of chancel-paving from the church and a cross-bar of 'Shakespeare's chair'. Mrs Hornby ran the birthplace from 1793 to 1820. (Sir Walter Scott came the summer after her retirement, and Carlyle three years after Scott.) By 1806 she was receiving a thousand visitors a year. No wonder Fitz-Gerald wrote, of his visit with Tennyson in June 1840: 'It was not the town itself, or even the church that touched me most, but the old footpaths over the fields which He must have crossed three centuries ago.'

FitzGerald habitually sprinkled his letters with capitals, but the 'He' is significant. In the birthplace, Tennyson 'was seized with a sort of enthusiasm' and scribbled his name among the hundreds upon the walls. (Scott's and Carlyle's are indelibly, though not very legibly, cut in the window-panes.) Tennyson was afterwards 'a little ashamed of it'. But they walked, as the true pilgrims do, the mile through the meadows to Shottery, to the house (Plate 5) where He went to court Anne Hathaway. The beautiful old house stands at right-angles to the road, which is bordered by a murmuring stream and a meadowful of cattle. It is very like Celia's home in *As You Like It*:

> West of this place, down in the neighbour bottom,
> The rank of osiers by the murmuring stream
> Left on your right hand brings you to the place.

The path from Stratford runs behind a remarkable series of black-and-white half-timbered cottages in Tavern Lane, Shottery. The back garden of one, called fancifully, but understandably, 'Wild Thyme', is especially idyllic, shaded deep green by elms, but lit by lilacs, aquilegias, and gaudy mauve stocks. The path flanks an old orchard, chest-deep in cow-parsley in June, and one remembers the exchange between husband and wife that always brought tears to Tennyson's eyes. It comes almost at the end of *Cymbeline*; as Imogen embraces him, Posthumus says:

> Hang there, like fruit, my soul,
> Till the tree die.

Soon after the third centenary of the birth, Henry James was in England, treading what he called 'the eternal stretched velvet' of Warwickshire. (The image is uncomfortably near to Dumaine's in his effort at an ode in *Love's Labour's Lost*:

> Through the velvet leaves the wind,
> All unseen, 'gan passage find.)

Henry James declared, and in doing so pointed directly at the difficulty about Shakespeare and Warwickshire: 'A great thought keeps you company as you go and gives character to the scenery. Warwickshire – you say it over and over – was Shakespeare's country.'

This 'great thought' induces too reverent an attitude. The bedroom, Hall's Croft, and Mary Arden's house at Wilmcote are all accepted too eagerly. Yet in Stratford and Warwickshire, beneath the 'relics' and the gleaming waxed-oak furniture, there remain in the streets and footpaths, the buildings and the old written records, enough clues to give reality to at least the circumstances of Shakespeare's life here, in aspiring youth and prosperous middle age, so that we know the kind of things he must have known, if not very much of the detail of what he specifically did. We certainly know enough to be able to rate as foolish and superfluous the whole Baconian creed. Yet, and this accounts for the existence of Baconianism, William Shakespeare continues to pass, in schoolrooms and other places of opportunity, as the old legendary figure that should have been destroyed by the researches of Edmond Malone (1741–1812).

The explanation of this is simple. The first biography, produced during the reign of Anne by Nicholas Rowe, a pot-boiling of legend and anecdote, is readable. It was reprinted. It established the almost universal myth of Shakespeare, 'born in a rude age and educated in the lowest manner', the son of a mere tradesman (usually a butcher, as with Cardinal Wolsey) who got into debt (he did, but no one else in this period fostered the town's interests for so many years or with more credit), so that the boy was taken early from school, apprenticed to his father, caught poaching on the neighbouring estate of Sir Thomas Lucy at Charlecote, thrashed, and forced to fly to London where he got a call-boy's job with a band of actors who discovered his literary talent. Furthermore this myth, almost totally removed from the truth, fitted in wonderfully with the ideas of the Romantic Movement. It is clear that Carlyle, for instance, mentally bracketed Shakespeare with his Scottish hero Burns, whose origins *were* rather humble, and with Homer, whose origins were unalterably traditional and impenetrably obscure. Against the forces of ignorance and the Romantic Movement, Shakespearian scholarship has so far made only the most preliminary advances.

Shakespeare was born in 1564 and christened in Stratford parish church on 26 April. His birthday is traditionally kept on 23 April (which was certainly his death-day in 1616) perhaps because three days was a likely lapse of time after birth, and partly because 23 April is St George's Day and Shakespeare is our national poet. This kind of coincidence has perhaps been more helpful to the legend than to the truth. In Shakespeare's life, there do at first sight appear to have been some of those coincidences associated with prophesied religions: the great national poet, celebrated on St George's Day, born in the earthen heart of England to a plain husbandman or tradesman and his wife called Mary Arden. Both the Ardens and the Shakespeares came from the gentle hills to the north of the Avon valley – his family from Snitterfield and hers from Wilmcote. Back in the Middle Ages the records certainly suggest that they both came from the heart of the Forest of Arden, which stretched up from Stratford through Henley-in-Arden, Tanworth-in-Arden (Tanworth had its maypole till a century ago), through Packwood and Meriden to Arbury, near Coventry and Nuneaton, the scene of George Eliot's novels. Arbury, where she was born, was originally Ardbury. Its common element with Arden probably means *earth*, the specially heavy kind of marl-earth on which the elm- and the oak-forest flourished. Mary Arden's grandfather was spelt *Arthurn* in a deed of 1504.

TOUCHSTONE: Is thy name William?
WILLIAM: William, sir.
TOUCHSTONE: A fair name. Wast born i' the forest here?
WILLIAM: Ay, sir, I thank God.

What is plain is that Shakespeare's father, John, moved down from Snitterfield, the village three miles north-west of Stratford, to work in the town. The names of various Shakespeares may be seen in the registers of the little church at Snitterfield. In 1535, a Richard Shakespeare of Snitterfield, probably William's grandfather, was charged with overburdening the common pasture with his cattle. Today one sees Frisian cattle at Snitterfield, grazing in the shade of a broad-spreading oak. The roads from Snitterfield down the slopes to Bishopton and Wilmcote run through tunnels of living oak. This Richard rented his Snitterfield house from Robert Arden of Wilmcote, whose daughter Mary married Shakespeare's father.

The 'Mary Arden House' at Wilmcote, maintained by the Shakespeare Birthplace Trust, may not be the Ardens' house: but that is no reason for not seeing it. It is a very good example of the sort of house Shakespeare's mother was brought up in – a prosperous farmhouse, nothing impoverished or mean. The youngest of eight daughters, she inherited land in Wilmcote called 'Asbyes'. Her father's house had painted cloth-hangings in hall and chamber, the stock included horses, sheep, swine, bees, and poultry; bacon hung in the roof.

The man she married, John Shakespeare, had already moved into Stratford – the critical decision for their son's future. John had never learnt to write, and always signed with his mark, a pair of glover's compasses. William did learn to read and write. One of the principal amenities for Stratford boys, then as now, was a grammar-school. We need not doubt that he went. His works may be taken as record enough.

It is not difficult to reconstruct Elizabethan Stratford in the mind, especially as one walks there. The town-plan is hardly altered (Plates 2 and 3). There were about 200 houses and perhaps 1,500 people. No less than a thousand elms were

growing in the town in 1582. It was very natural for Shakespeare to think of these elegantly-clad, tall, noble trees in
metaphors like Adriana's in *The Comedy of Errors*: 'Thou
art an elm, my husband'. Though not recorded, there would
certainly be many willows 'aslant' the Avon and its tribu-
taries, as there are now, pale-green feather fans beside Clopton Bridge (Plate 6a). It may not be irrelevant to Ophelia's
fate that at Tiddington, about a mile above Clopton Bridge,
one Katherine Hamlet was drowned late in 1579; the
coincidence of names is extraordinary.

Stratford means 'street-ford', the place where the Roman
road from Droitwich and Alcester crossed the Avon, and
upon which seven main roads now converge. By the thir-
teenth century, when Stratford had been granted its market
and fairs, there was a wooden bridge. By 1500, the present
splendid stone bridge had been given by Sir Hugh Clopton,
of Clopton House, a Lord Mayor of London. This bridge
and the church attest the prosperity of the market-town by
the beginning of the sixteenth century. The splendid stone-
panelled, clerestoried nave (Plate 10) stands comparison
with that at the celebrated clothing-town of Long Melford
in Suffolk. The font is a modern copy of the one in which
Shakespeare was baptized. Remains of the original were
discovered on a near-by rockery.

From Clopton Bridge, Bridge Street rises, broad and
breezy, with an air of regattas in the summer, and is the
most changed of all the streets since Shakespeare's time.
Then, the top half of the street was divided down the middle
by Middle Row, a row of some of the most important shops
in the town. At the bottom of the street stood two of the
town's chief inns, the Bear on the left, the Swan on the
right, now the site of the Mulberry Tree. The Market-House
was at the top, roughly where Barclay's Bank rears its
cupola.

Henley Street, curving off to the right, led to Henley-in-

Arden, and in it Shakespeare was born. His father, John, was now established as a glover and whittawer (tawer of skins into 'whit' leather, a saddler). They had the chief stall-site in the market, and he was soon Stratford's chief townsman, Alderman in 1565 and Bailiff in 1568. It is notable that the first record of professional players visiting the town occurred in 1569, during John's term of office; which argues that he was well-disposed towards the theatre. William's birth was most fortunately timed: by 1602, puritanism was prevalent and plays forbidden in Stratford. Official performances would be in the guildhall, others at inns; at the Bear, for example. William would certainly have seen them, and here in Stratford he could have joined one of the companies. In the summer of 1587 the Queen's Men were short of an actor (one had slain another). Next year Leicester's company was short of several; they were touring abroad.

'The Birthplace' was Shakespeare's home as a boy, though of course he may have been born in any of the bedrooms (Plate 8a). To the right, as you face the house, stood the tenement of William Wedgewood, a tailor, and right of that (the Birthplace Trust's present office) was the smithy of Richard Hornby, perhaps an ancestor of that Mrs Hornby's husband who kept the Birthplace in the Regency period. He made links and staples 'for the sergeants to make fast their prisoners'.

In September 1575, the tailor was 'compelled to go from Stratford', where he had been living with a woman not his wife, and start up again in Warwick. He was ill received there by the Earl of Warwick, who wrote from the Court at Woodstock that, for his dishonest living, Wedgewood was 'afore banished by my commandment'. We see how readily the peremptory language of kings and noblemen would early in Shakespeare's life be accessible to Henley Street in Stratford. Indeed John Shakespeare had been in Westminster three years before, suing successfully in the

Court of Common Pleas on the town's behalf. So much for the legend of Shakespeare's impossibly poor start in life.

At Warwick, incidentally, the Beauchamp Chapel in St Mary's church contains the tomb of Richard Beauchamp, Earl of Warwick, the sarcophagus bearing the most magnificent brazen effigy outside Westminster Abbey. It is just possible that Shakespeare was thinking of it when, in his early play *Love's Labour's Lost*, he made the King open with:

> Let fame, that all hunt after in their lives,
> Live registered upon our brazen tombs.

Later, in 2 *Henry IV*, Shakespeare gave some of his best-remembered lines to that Earl of Warwick:

> There is a history in all men's lives,
> Figuring the nature of the times deceased;
> The which observed, a man may prophesy,
> With a near aim, of the main chance of things
> As yet not come to life.

No one has better defined the uses and the limitations of history.

In 1575, William's twelfth year, the Queen made her sensational summer visit to Warwick and Kenilworth. Kenilworth Castle was the seat she had given ten years earlier to her favourite, Leicester. She arrived on 9 July, and stayed eighteen golden days. 'This gift did Jupiter confer upon Her Highness, to have fair and reasonable weather at command', a priceless gift in an English July. Leicester, too, lavished all his riches and all his ostentatious devotion. To the ancient fortress he had added 'Leicester's Building', a soaring block with vast vertical mullioned windows (Plate 7a) on the grandiose scale that Bess of Hardwick rivalled at the end of the reign. Some of Leicester's new chambers, including perhaps the Queen's bedchamber, had side views out over the unruffled lake. As she arrived, that first evening, a floating island, sparkling with lights, moved over the water towards her, bearing a nereid in silken dress, who in a boy's treble told her that he was 'the Lady of this pleasant lake', and that 'The Lake, the Lodge, the Lord, are yours for to command'.

Next day, Sunday, she watched part of the performance by the men of Coventry of a local traditional play called *The Slaughter of the Danes at Hock Tide*. There wasn't time to finish the performance, but she said it was so good that she must see the whole of it next Tuesday. It is impossible not to remember Theseus's response, towards the end of Bottom's staggering production of *Pyramus and Thisbe*: 'No epilogue, I pray you; for your play needs no excuse ...'

> The iron tongue of midnight hath told twelve;
> Lovers to bed ...
> A fortnight hold we this solemnity,
> In nightly revels and new jollity.

Every day, and late into the night, the precincts and park were crowded with three or four thousand of the people of Warwickshire, determined to see and to entertain her. On the hot evening of 18 July Her Highness remained indoors until five o'clock, and then rode forth, a Diana, to hunt. On her return from Chase Wood and the Pleasance (to the left of Plate 7a) she came to the bridge and there witnessed a new display of *The Lady of the Lake*. Triton rode on 'a swimming mermaid', blowing his horn. Later, the distressed Lady of the Lake drew near on a flotilla of moving islands with her nymphs, followed by Arion wearing a horse's head mask and riding on a dolphin's back. Confronted at the bridge by the proud Queen on horseback, Arion forgot his lines and dried up. Finally, pulling off his head-gear in desperation, he shouted 'he was none of Arion, not he, but honest Harry Goldingham'. The Queen must

1. Stratford-upon-Avon: the Town Hall and Chapel Street, looking towards the site of New Place and the Guild Chapel.

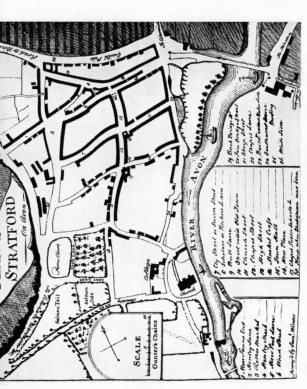

3. The earliest plan of Stratford-upon-Avon, by Samuel Winter, 1759. (Note the unchanged layout of the major streets.)

4. Shakespeare's Warwickshire: a cottage at Hampton Lucy.

5. The Hathaway House, Shottery, traditionally the home of Shakespeare's wife.

6a. Clopton Bridge, Stratford-upon-Avon; built late in the fifteenth century.

6b. Mason's Court in Rother Street, Stratford-upon-Avon.

7a. Kenilworth Castle as it appeared in 1620. From an early nineteenth-century engraving of a lost painting.

Deare tobit tobies leat, to ye litte or ragea for mone hat sed

7b. Part of the wall-painting in the White Swan Hotel, Stratford-upon-Avon, showing a scene from the Book of Tobit (painted

8b. Harvard House, Stratford-upon-Avon, home of Katherine Rogers, mother of John Harvard, the

8a. A bedroom in the Shakespeare House in Henley Street, Stratford-upon-Avon (Shakespeare's birthplace).

GOOD FREND FOR IESVS SAKE FORBEARE
TO DIGG THE DVST ENCLOASED HEARE
BLESE BE Y MAN Y SPARES HES STONES
AND CVRST BE HE Y MOVES MY BONES

9b. Shakespeare's gravestone.

9a. Shakespeare's monument in Holy Trinity Church.

10. The nave of Holy Trinity Church, Stratford-upon-Avon.

11. The garden and site of New Place, Shakespeare's last home, overlooking the Guild Chapel.

12b. Henry Wriothesley, third Earl of Southampton.
Portrait by an unknown artist about 1614, when

12a. Queen Elizabeth in her coronation robes; an anonymous
painting probably of 1559 (Warwick Castle)

have been every bit as familiar with Bottom as Shakespeare was; with Bottom translated, and especially with Bottom in the original.

The son of a local dignitary, Shakespeare is more than likely to have been present at some of the festivities at Kenilworth, even to have taken part in them. Later, when he wrote *A Midsummer Night's Dream*, he addressed, it is suggested, a private evocation to one of the courtiers who had attended the Queen at Kenilworth.

> Thou rememberest
> Since once I sat upon a promontory
> And heard a mermaid on a dolphin's back ...
> And certain stars shot madly from their spheres
> To hear the sea-maid's music ...
> Cupid all arm'd: a certain aim he took
> At a fair vestal throned by the west ...
> And the imperial votaress passed on,
> In maiden meditation, fancy-free.

In Shakespeare's day it was natural and commonplace to act out scenes of ancient local history like *The Slaughter of the Danes at Hock Tide*, and also to enact guild pageants, the scenes of religious history. Such stories had for centuries appeared to people in paintings all over the walls and in the windows of their churches, some of the murals being painted as late as the reign of Mary Tudor, whom Elizabeth succeeded six years before Shakespeare's birth. Obliterated by whitewash in the circumstances of Elizabeth's church settlement, they may still have appeared on some secular walls. At Stratford, in the Rother Market, round the corner from the Shakespeares' house, in a tavern known as the King's Hall, and now the White Swan Hotel, a wall-painting of about 1560 depicts scenes from the Apocryphal story of Tobias and the angel (Plate 7b).

The picture is singularly like the coloured sketch for a

stage-set. Appropriately prophetic, it shows a sort of pros-cenium-stage, with the young Jew Tobias in the costume fashionable in the days of Shakespeare's youth, being sent off from Nineveh to collect his father's money in Media. To be actually translated into the language of the theatre, the theme had to wait for James Bridie in the 1930s. But the mere fact that it was painted on a wall just round the corner from Shakespeare's home is interesting. It is an example of one form of stimulus that was certainly present in a Strat-ford tavern in the days when the young dramatist's mind was being formed. The strength of the stimuli may perhaps be measured by the range and wisdom and poetry of Gaunt's advice to the banished Bolingbroke in contrast with the prosy commandments Tobias received from his father in the Apocryphal *Book of Tobit*.

Along Rother Street from the Rother Market (it was the cattle-market: 'rother' means ox), Mason's Court (Plate 6b) is the best, because least restored, example of a small town-house from Shakespeare's time. Now two tenements, it was built, probably in the fifteenth century, as one house with an open two-storey hall in the middle, the ends divided into upper and lower rooms. Harvard House (Plate 8b) in High Street, is an altogether grander affair, rebuilt after the fire of 1594 by Thomas Rogers, a butcher and great buyer of barley and of cattle. (Stratford was ravaged by fire in 1594, 1595, and again in 1614.) Katherine Rogers, one of his many chil-dren, became the mother of John Harvard, founder of the distinguished American university.

Shakespeare's own acquaintance with the fairs of the neighbourhood (it would seem distinctly odd in Francis Bacon), is demonstrated by the interview between Shallow and his servant Davy in 2 *Henry IV*, in which Davy asks: 'Sir, do you mean to stop any of William's wages, about the sack he lost the other day at Hinckley fair?' At Hinckley, in Leicestershire, just across the Warwickshire border, a

'Shew Fair' was regularly held on Whit-Monday. (It was revived in the 1780s after a lapse of forty years, but soon fell again into disuse.) A large number of millers assembled from the neighbouring villages, and put on a 'shew' in cavalcade. At another point about a mile or so beyond the Roman Watling Street which divides Leicestershire from Warwickshire, in May 1607, 'full five thousand' hungry, impoverished rioters assembled at Cotesbach 'to level and lay open inclosures' of the ancient open fields of Cotesbach. They were men of Warwickshire, Northamptonshire, and Leicestershire, many of them dispossessed by enclosures like this latest one by a rich London draper and government contractor. Shakespeare was writing *Coriolanus* about this time. It has been remarked that one of the defects of *Coriolanus* is the extent to which Shakespeare followed the translator of Plutarch, and that one clear variant from the original is the opening of Shakespeare's play with a row in Rome about 'hunger for bread'. In Plutarch the rumpus is about usury.

Not far from Harvard House in Stratford, along Chapel Street, and on the corner immediately opposite the medieval guild-chapel, guildhall, and grammar-school, is the site of New Place (Plate 11). In 1597 its owner William Underhill was poisoned by his son, who was executed. Shakespeare thereupon bought the house for £60, and made it the family seat. He had buried his only son, Hamnet, the previous year:

> Grief fills the room up of my absent child,
> Lies in his bed, walks up and down with me.
>
> *(King John)*

Now he helped his father to acquire a coat of arms (Plate 15) and provided one of the best houses in Stratford. Over the following years, several members of the family seem to have lived in it, jointly or successively. In 1602, Shakespeare

bought 107 acres of land (presumably arable) and 20 of
pasture for £320, and invested £440 in a lease of tithes that
brought him in £60 a year. Among the rest of the Stratford
tittle-tattle about Shakespeare recorded a generation later by
the Restoration vicar, there was a rumour, for what it is
worth, that 'in his elder days ... he spent at the rate of
£1,000 a year'.

So it is a prosperous and marvellously fulfilled genius, a
Prospero well established in the society of Stratford, a con-
vivial celebrity, with a wide circle of friends, who looks out
from his bust (Plate 9a) in the chancel of the church where
he was baptized and buried. As true a countryman as Corin,
'glad of other men's good, content with my own', his wide-
open eyes have a distant look; he knew that 'we are such
stuff as dreams are made on'. This effigy is the work of the
younger Gerard Johnson, one of the leading London
sculptors. His family's workshop was in Southwark, where
Shakespeare's figure was very well known. The bust is the
only convincing picture of him left.

Beneath it, in the rich earth of Arden, lies the grave.
Prospero's valediction provides a notable link in form with
the lines carved on the gravestone (Plate 9b).

> Now my charms are all o'erthrown,
> And what strength I have's mine own ...
> As you from crimes would pardon'd be,
> Let your indulgence set me free.

This is not incompatible, metrically or in spirit, with

> Good friend, for Jesus' sake forbear
> To dig the dust enclosèd here.

These lines on the gravestone are perhaps the last he com-
posed. They express a dread, not uncommon in his day, lest
his bones be moved and himself disturbed in the sleep that

rounds our little life. They conclude with a curse, so far effective:

> Blest be the man that spares these stones,
> And curst be he that moves my bones.

Soon after his death there was a proposal to bring the remains away from Warwickshire for re-burial in Westminster Abbey. At such an idea, Ben Jonson, his drinking-companion in that reported celebration a few days before the end of his life, exclaimed:

> My Shakespeare, rise! I will not lodge thee by
>   Chaucer or Spenser, or bid Beaumont lie
> A little further, to make thee a room;
>   Thou art a monument without a tomb,
> And art alive still while thy book doth live,
>   And we have wits to read and praise to give.

SHAKESPEARE'S
LONDON

Charles J. Sisson

HAT did London mean to Shakespeare? We know how much Stratford-upon-Avon meant to him. The record of his life begins with the entry in the extant parish register of Holy Trinity Church of his baptism there on 26 April 1564, and ends with his burial in the chancel of the church on 25 April 1616. He was a Midlander and a provincial, from the heart of England, almost exactly from its centre of gravity. He sought his career in London, the centre of the social and political life of England, which offered opportunities for making a fortune to ambitious young men from the provinces, who nevertheless remained obstinately provincial, as did Shakespeare and a hundred others. Their ambitions were fulfilled when they had adorned churches and endowed schools in their native counties, as Shakespeare enhanced the reputation of his family in New Place. In London, the records show us only a Shakespeare who sought comfort in lodgings with French Huguenots, the Mountjoys, in Silver Street – lodgings in London, but a great house in Stratford for his wife and family. The most misleading entry in a *cursus vitae* of William Shakespeare is the universally accepted date of 1610 for the 'Probable

Migration of Shakespeare to Stratford' (E. K. Chambers, *William Shakespeare*, 11, xiv), where since 1597 he had been the householder of New Place. It is a deep-rooted modern fallacy that London was not readily accessible from Stratford, nor Stratford from London, at any rate to the Elizabethans who resided in them or had business in them. A Londoner nowadays, with aeroplanes, railways, and motor-cars at his service may well look upon the prospect of a visit to Stratford with greater trepidation than Shakespeare upon the roads of his day, busy with horsemen and waggons upon their daily journeys. We shall be nearer the truth if we look upon London as Shakespeare's place of business, and Stratford as his home, throughout his life.

The impact of London upon Shakespeare, when he first broke into this market for talent, should not be exaggerated. Its unfamiliarity had been discounted for him by the experience of Midland youth making their way by apprenticeship in the guilds of London craftsmen and business men. It is significant that his early volumes of poetry were printed and published by a London stationer of Stratford origin, Richard Field. The world of the City might well be familiar to him from reports from such men. The world of the Court, on the other hand, might present a spectacle of the unknown. Yet we find Shakespeare, in his early days as a dramatist, apparently familiar with the behaviour and discourse of Court circles, as in *A Midsummer Night's Dream* and *Love's Labour's Lost*. We may be inclined to accept a recent conjecture (Rosemary Anne Sisson, *The Young Shakespeare*, 1961) that his early days were spent as a page in the house of Sir Fulke Greville, near Stratford, at Beauchamp Court, the centre of a cultured literary society, and that there, rather than at King Edward's grammar-school at Stratford, he had his literary and social education and became familiar with the ways of the great. An obvious parallel is Michael Drayton, poet and dramatist, of the same age as Shakespeare, of similar family circumstances, and from the same county, whom we know to have been a page in the house of Sir Henry Goodere at Polesworth at the age of ten, and later in the service of other members of the family before he pursued a literary career. Such men, like the Queen herself, had schoolmasters in their service.

It is at all events apparent that in Shakespeare's approach to London the world of the Court and of literary society loomed larger than the world of the City, in which he never sought material for his plays. His only comedy of middle-class life has its scene laid in Windsor, and was designed by royal command to afford fresh scope for his comic knight Falstaff. His London worlds were the world of the Court and of the Inns of Court with their common passion for literature and the drama, and the world of the theatre to which he devoted his ambition and in which he made his fortune. His London was indeed an aristocratic urban society above all, of advanced literary tastes which his earlier work is plainly designed to please and with marked success. The City had nothing to offer him except the services of printers and publishers in a market in which literature drowned in a flood of works of theological content. Its policy was utterly opposed to the profession of the stage. The Lord Mayors of London, on its behalf, waged a continuous war against the theatre, using their own powers within the City, and seeking the support of the Queen's Privy Council for its suppression everywhere. The Court, on the other hand, gave its patronage to the actors and their plays, and fees for performances at Court were among their chief sources of income, authorized by the Queen herself as by her successor James I, both great lovers of the acted drama. There too could be sought, and found, patrons for such poetical work as formed part of the ambitions of Shakespeare and Drayton alike for a literary career. In 1593 Shakespeare was permitted to dedicate *Venus and Adonis* to the Earl of Southampton

(Plate 12b), who encouraged him a year later to dedicate to him *The Rape of Lucrece* (see page 34). It is plain enough where his interests lay in his approach to London.

We do not know when Shakespeare first visited London on his search for a career as actor, poet, and dramatist, except that it must have been much earlier than is generally accepted, and that it is absurd to conceive of a career as dramatist that did not begin until 1592, at the age of twenty-eight. But it is clear that he would see London essentially as we see it in retrospect today. There were three Londons open to his view.

There was the City, tightly packed and prosperous within its walls and gates, with its centre in St Paul's Cathedral, and with the numerous spires of its parish churches rising above the narrow streets (Plate 13). The Halls of its Guilds gave importance to its craftsmen, and the great Guildhall itself bore witness to the whole might of London, the concentration of a powerful economic and social unity. It had its own aristocracy of Aldermen and Councillors, of Masters and Wardens of Companies, and at its head the Lord Mayor and the Sheriffs, the governors of this crowded world within the City Bars. Its civic virtues were obedience to authority, excellence in a chosen craft or occupation, and devotion to family life, with which were allied a deep loyalty to the Crown and the faithful practice of the religion established by law. The rewards of civic life were promotion within this society and the accumulation of wealth. The recurring symbols of civic splendour were the great feasts of the Guilds and the City held in state in their halls, and the annual pageants of the Guilds, of which the Lord Mayor's Show alone survives today.

Hard by the City, west of Ludgate, and along the Thames, was the second world of Westminster, the Strand with its great houses of prelates and noblemen, the Inns of Court where the law was studied in what was then known as the

TO THE RIGHT
HONOVRABLE, HENRY
VVriothesley, Earle of Southhampton,
and Baron of Titchfield.

THE loue I dedicate to your Lordship is without end:wherof this Pamphlet without beginning is but a superfluous Moity. The warrant I haue of your Honourable disposition, not the worth of my vntutord Lines makes it assured of acceptance. VVhat I haue done is yours, what I haue to doe is yours, being part in all I haue, deuoted yours. VVere my worth greater, my duety would shew greater, meane time, as it is, it is bound to your Lordship; To whom I with long life still lengthned with all happinesse.

Your Lordships in all duety.

William Shakespeare.

A 2

The dedication of *The Rape of Lucrece* (1594)

Third University, the University of London, and Whitehall, the seat of the Crown, with royal palaces, offices of State, courts of law, and the Houses of Parliament. History and tradition were enshrined in its great Church, Westminster Abbey. Further down the river Tower Hill stood high, with the Tower of London frowning over the citizens, the citadel of the ultimate royal power whose gates closed upon Thomas More, the Earl of Essex, and Sir Walter Raleigh in turn, to await death at the hands of that sovereign justice which was beyond the law, a symbol of terror to all men. The roaring of the lions kept in the Tower for men to wonder at, the first London Zoo, might well recall the memory of their former dread sovereign King Henry VIII, his voice still audible in Lion Tower.

Shakespeare had little occasion for familiarity with the world of the City, as far as we can see. Its great inns in Bishopsgate and Ludgate may have offered him temporary abode. Its apprentices, with the young lawyers of the Inns of Court, furnished much of his audiences for his plays in public theatres. And when he printed his poems, he would need to call upon Richard Field in Paul's Churchyard, at the sign of the White Greyhound. But the world of the Court called for his daily attention in the pursuit of his profession, which depended for very existence upon its protection. He and his fellows were servants of the Lord Chamberlain, until they came under the patronage of the King himself, and walked in procession in the King's livery at his coronation in Westminster Abbey. The Master of the Revels controlled for his master, the Lord Chamberlain, the affairs of the professional theatre, and chose plays for performance at Court by various companies of professional actors, with his favour ensured for the company in which Shakespeare was a sharer. The traffic with the Revels office and its Master Tilney was dense, with plays submitted for licence or for performance at Court, theatres to be licensed annually, and other needs, all involving fees at every step to the Master and his officers in Whitehall. There too was the Exchequer, where the actors' leaders called with warrants for payment for Court performances, again with fees by way of commission to smooth the way. It is perhaps characteristic that Shakespeare's only known appearance in a court of law is as a witness in the Royal Prerogative Court of Requests, which held its sittings in Whitehall, in territory far more familiar to him than the world of the City, and more closely allied to him by common affairs and indeed by vested interests on both sides.

The third world presented to Shakespeare by London was the world of the theatre, a far-flung world remote from City and Court alike, in the suburbs. It embraced Bankside and Paris Garden on the south side of the Thames, accessible on foot across Tower Bridge or by wherry on the water, as its main seat; with the Rose, the Hope, the Swan, and Shakespeare's Globe. The northern suburbs of Shoreditch and Clerkenwell had the earliest known buildings erected for the professional stage in the Theatre and the Curtain in 1576, followed by such famous theatres as the Fortune and the Red Bull. London's theatre-land extended to the east, beyond Aldgate, into Whitechapel, from the beginning of Elizabeth's reign, in the Boar's Head and the Red Lion, inns converted into playing-houses with permanent structures, in the next parish to Shoreditch.

The City, in the days of Henry VIII, had been a mainstay, with the Court, of the infant professional stage. At the end of its feasts the guests were entertained by plays performed by professional actors. But the impact of the Puritan reformers of religion brought them into conflict with the stage and drama. The great City inns of Bishopsgate and Ludgate had once been centres of professional acting, with their yards converted into theatres. The Bell and the Bull had been the winter theatres of the Queen's Men in 1583, and Shakespeare's own company used the Cross Keys in Gracechurch Street as late as 1594 as a winter headquarters, doubtless between provincial tours. But the actors had long laboured under the determined opposition of civic authority, which achieved in 1596 the final closing of the City inns to theatrical activities, together with the banishment of the theatres to the suburbs. A minor part of the world of the stage nearer the City was the exceptional 'private theatre', with the child-actors of St Paul's who acted Lyly's plays, and the first and second Blackfriars, the second a companion house to Shakespeare's Globe, both indoor theatres designed for select audiences from the Court and Inns of Court. But the theatre-world proper as it thus developed lay along the main roads entering London from the south, from the north, and from the east, in the great suburbs of crowded, increasing population, and yielding an open market for the professional entertainment offered by the actors, in comparative freedom from the control of the hostile City of London.

The theatres themselves were among the sights of London, celebrated in the diaries of foreign visitors to England for the splendour of their structure, the costumes of their actors, and the excellence of their performances. We owe to a Dutch visitor, de Witt, the only representation we possess of the interior of such a theatre, the Swan on Bankside (reproduced on p. 38). The preliminary preparations for normal performances began at eleven in the morning, and they took place after midday dinner and by daylight. All London indeed obeyed the clock, in the absence of street-lighting, and rose with the sun, whose setting emptied the crowded, busy streets and left them to darkness and to the watchmen with their lanterns, no fit places indeed, in City or suburbs alike, for the world of the theatre to serve the needs of their patrons.

The world of the City described Shakespeare and his fellows, in an official letter from the Lord Mayor to the

The Swan Theatre, London: the drawing by Johannes de Witt about 1596

Lord Chancellor, 'the players of plays and tumblers and such like', as 'a very superfluous sort of men' (E. K. Chambers, *The Elizabethan Stage*, IV, 279). But at Court the great Earls of Pembroke and Montgomery were the patrons of the First Folio of Shakespeare's plays. And his friend Ben Jonson, actor and dramatist, shared with Chaucer and Spenser the honour of burial in Westminster Abbey itself. Truly it may seem that the world of the Court under Elizabeth and James, rather than the world of the City of London, stood for the true freedom and splendour of humanity and art, which unite all races of men bound together by the genius of Shakespeare.

SHAKESPEARE AS SEEN
BY HIS CONTEMPORARIES

T. J. B. Spencer

HAKESPEARE made a strong impression upon his contemporaries. But they saw him as one of themselves and praised him, not as a unique phenomenon, but in relation to other writers of the time. The allusions to Shakespeare in his lifetime are fairly numerous – if one takes into consideration his station in society and the slight survival value of private documents in a world in which there was an acute shortage of paper for domestic uses. What was said about him builds up a picture of a friendly, cooperative, easily successful and therefore not self-assertive, personality.

Yet the first certain allusion to Shakespeare in print is apparently an envious sneer at a brilliant newcomer to the literary and theatrical scene. In 1592, when Shakespeare was 28, there was published *Greene's Groatsworth of Wit, Bought with a Million of Repentance*. Here Robert Greene gives satirical advice to his friends who 'spend their wits in making plays'. The actors, he says, take over the plays from authors and make use of them solely for their own profit.

Yes, trust them not. For there is an upstart crow, beautified with our feathers, that with his 'Tiger's heart wrapped in a player's hide' supposes he is as well able to bombast out a blank verse as the best of you; and, being an absolute *Johannes Factotum*, is in his own conceit the only Shake-scene in a country. O that I might entreat your rare wits to be employed in more profitable courses.

This is an obscure passage. But the reference to 'Shake-scene' and the parody of a line in one of the most famous speeches in the second part of *Henry VI*

O tiger's heart wrapped in a woman's hide!

make it certain that Shakespeare is the object of Greene's sarcasm. The book was published after Greene's death, and a mutual acquaintance (Henry Chettle) tried to undo the damage by making an apology and asserting Shakespeare's respectability and literary merit.

Myself have seen his demeanour no less civil than he excellent in the quality he professes. Besides, divers of worship have reported his uprightness of dealing, which argues his honesty, and his facetious grace in writing, that approves his art.

Henry Chettle, a well-meaning impecunious author, is smoothing down the clever young man, who has influential friends ('divers of worship') and a rising position in the theatrical world, as well as noticeable artistic merit.

Subsequently, throughout Shakespeare's lifetime, there was nothing comparable to Greene's derogatory remarks. In 1598 when Shakespeare was 34, Francis Meres of Pembroke College, Cambridge, published a curious book entitled *Palladis Tamia, or, Wit's Treasury*, which includes a kind of survey of the literary and artistic situation; and for him Shakespeare is clearly already in the front rank of modern writers:

The English tongue is mightily enriched and gorgeously invested in rare ornaments and resplendent habiliments by Sir Philip Sidney, Spenser, Daniel, Drayton, Warner, Shakespeare, Marlowe, and Chapman.

Meres's method of praising English authors is to compare them with the great Greek, Latin, and Italian poets of the past who wrote in similar kinds:

> The sweet witty soul of Ovid lives in mellifluous and honey-tongued Shakespeare. Witness his *Venus and Adonis*, his *Lucrece*, his sugared Sonnets among his private friends, etc.

For an Elizabethan, especially for a classically-educated man like Meres, the Latin dramatists, Plautus, Terence, and Seneca, provided the standard of comparison; and Shakespeare is their rival as a playwright:

> As Plautus and Seneca are accounted the best for comedy and tragedy among the Latins, so Shakespeare among the English is the most excellent in both kinds for the stage. For comedy, witness his *Gentleman of Verona*, his *Errors*, his *Love's Labour's Lost*, his *Love's Labour's Won* [whatever that may have been], his *Midsummer-Night's Dream*, and his *Merchant of Venice*. For tragedy, his *Richard the Second, Richard the Third, Henry the Fourth, King John, Titus Andronicus*, and his *Romeo and Juliet.* (The relevant page of Meres's book is reproduced opposite.)

This was a splendid compliment to a young man (at this time, 1598, most of Shakespeare's best plays were not yet written) and Meres continues with an approbation of Shakespeare's style: 'I say that the Muses would speak with Shakespeare's fine-filed phrase, if they would speak English.'

Some of the plays mentioned by Meres had not yet been printed; so he must have derived his impressions from stage-productions. Other playgoers, too, begin to allude to episodes in Shakespeare's plays which had been specially effective on the stage. John Weever, of Queen's College, Cambridge, a minor poet, plainly alludes in a poem he published in 1601 to a celebrated scene in *Julius Caesar*:

> The many-headed multitude were drawn
> By Brutus' speech that Caesar was ambitious.
> When eloquent Mark Antony had shown
> His virtues, who but Brutus then was vicious?

among his priuate friends,&c.

As *Plautus* and *Seneca* are accounted the best for Comedy and Tragedy among the Latines : so *Shakespeare* among ÿ English is the most excellent in both kinds for the stage; for Comedy, witnes his *Gētlemē of Verona*, his *Errors*, his *Loue labors lost*, his *Loue labours wonne*, his *Midsummers night dreame*, & his *Merchant of Venice*: for Tragedy his *Richard the 2. Richard the 3. Henry the 4. King Iohn, Titus Andronicus* and his *Romeo* and *Iuliet*.

As *Epius Stolo* said, that the Muses would speake with *Plautus* tongue, if they would speak Latin: so I say that the Muses would speak with *Shakespeares* fine filed phrase, if they would speake English.

As *Musæus*, who wrote the loue of *Hero* and *Leander*, had two excellent schollers, *Thamarus* & *Hercules*: so hath he in England two excellent Poets, imitators of him in the same argument and subiect, *Christopher Marlow*, and *George Chapman*.

As *Ouid* saith of his worke;

Iamꝗ opus exegi, quod nec Iouis ira, nec ignis,
Nec poterit ferrum, nec edax abolere vetustas.

And as *Horace* saith of his; *Exegi monumentū ære perennius; Regaliꝗ; situ pyramidū altius; Quod non imber edax; Non Aquilo impotens possit diruere; aut innumerabilis*

Oo2. *amnorum*

We have interesting references to other performances; to *The Comedy of Errors* at Gray's Inn on 28 December 1594:

The next grand night ... the Ambassador came ... about nine of the clock at night. ... There arose such a disordered tumult and crowd upon the stage that there was no opportunity to effect that which was intended. ... It was thought good not to offer anything of account, saving dancing and revelling with gentlewomen. And after such sports, a *Comedy of Errors* (like to Plautus his *Menaechmi*) was played by the players. So that night was begun and continued to the end in nothing but confusion and errors; whereupon it was ever afterwards called 'The Night of Errors'.

A young lawyer of the Middle Temple, John Manningham, kept a diary of his experiences in 1602 and 1603. On 2 February 1602 he records:

At our feast we had a play called *Twelfth Night, or What You Will*, much like the *Comedy of Errors* or *Menaechmi* in Plautus, but most like and near to that in Italian called *Inganni*. A good practice in it to make the steward believe his lady widow was in love with him, by counterfeiting a letter as from his lady in general terms, telling him what she liked best in him and prescribing his gesture in smiling, his apparel, etc., and then, when he came to practise, making him believe they took him to be mad.

It is John Manningham who tells an anecdote that was in circulation about Shakespeare and Richard Burbage, the great tragic actor of Shakespeare's company (13 March 1602).

Upon a time when Burbage played Richard III there was a citizen grew so far in liking with him that before she went from the play she appointed him to come that night unto her by name of 'Richard the Third'. Shakespeare, overhearing their conclusion, went before, was entertained, and at his game ere Burbage came. Then, message being brought that Richard the Third was at the door, Shakespeare caused return to be made that William the Conqueror was before Richard the Third.

Another recorder of his visits to the theatre was Simon Forman, who in 1611 saw productions of *Macbeth, Cymbeline,* and *The Winter's Tale* at the Globe. His accounts are remarkably full, as for example his impression of *The Winter's Tale* on 15 May 1611:

Observe there how Leontes, the king of Sicilia, was overcome with jealousy of his wife with the king of Bohemia, his friend that came to see him; and how he contrived his death and would have had his cupbearer to have poisoned; who gave the king of Bohemia warning thereof, and fled with him to Bohemia. Remember also how he sent to the oracle of Apollo, and the answer of Apollo: that she was guiltless, and that the king was jealous, etc., and how, except the child was found again that was lost, the king should die without issue. For the child was carried into Bohemia and there laid in a forest, and brought up by a shepherd. And the king of Bohemia his son married that wench. And how they fled into Sicilia to Leontes; and the shepherd having showed the letter of the nobleman by whom Leontes sent away that child, and the jewels found about her, she was known to be Leontes' daughter, and was then sixteen years old.

Remember also the rogue that came in all tattered like Coll Pixey; and how he feigned him sick and to have been robbed of all that he had: and how he cozened the poor man of all his money; and after came to the sheep-shear with a pedlar's pack and there cozened them again of all their money; and how he changed apparel with the king of Bohemia his son; and then how he turned courtier, etc. Beware of trusting feigned beggars or fawning fellows.

Clearly the character of Autolycus in the play made a strong impression upon Simon Forman when he saw Shakespeare's latest play at the Globe.

But the famous theatre was not to last much longer. On 2 July 1613 Sir Henry Wotton wrote a letter to Sir Edmund Bacon giving an account of the disastrous fire which broke out during a performance of Shakespeare's *Henry VIII*:

I will entertain you at the present with what has happened this week at the Bankside. The King's players had a new play, called *All is True*, representing some principal pieces of the reign of Henry VIII, which was set forth with many extra-ordinary circumstances of pomp and majesty, even to the matting of the stage; the Knights of the Order with their Georges and Garters, the guards with their embroidered coats, and the like; sufficient in truth within a while to make greatness very familiar, if not ridiculous. Now, King Henry making a masque at the Cardinal Wolsey's house, and certain chambers being shot off at his entry, some of the paper, or other stuff, wherewith one of them was stopped, did light on the thatch, where being thought at first but an idle smoke, and their eyes more attentive to the show, it kindled inwardly and ran round like a train, consuming within less than an hour the whole house, to the very grounds. This was the fatal period of that virtuous fabric, wherein yet nothing did perish but wood and straw, and a few forsaken cloaks. Only one man had his breeches set on fire, that would perhaps have broiled him, if he had not by the benefit of a provident wit put it out with bottle ale.

These first-hand accounts of performances of Shake-peare's plays in his own lifetime bring us close to Shake-speare's own experiences in his theatre. He does not appear to have been an outstanding actor himself. Later traditions attributed to him the parts of the Ghost in *Hamlet* and Adam in *As You Like It*. Neither of these is a long or de-manding part. But he seems to have been complimented for his taking the 'kingly parts' in plays. There is a verse-epigram by John Davies of Hereford, published in *The Scourge of Folly* in 1610, which is addressed 'To our English Terence, Mr Will. Shakespeare':

> Some say (good Will), which I in sport do sing,
> Had'st thou not played some kingly parts in sport,
> Thou had'st been a companion for a king,
> And been a king among the meaner sort.
> Some others rail. But, rail as they think fit,
> Thou hast no railing, but a reigning, wit.

Shakespeare's name appears in two actors' lists attached to Ben Jonson's plays: *Every Man in his Humour* (1598) and *Sejanus* (1603); and he heads the list of twenty-six named in the Folio edition of his plays in 1623 (see page 48). Perhaps he gave up regular acting because he was more advantageously employed writing plays for his company. He produced more than a million words in twenty years of writing life. This, together with administrative responsibilities for the theatre in which he was a shareholder, may not have left much time for acting.

Among Shakespeare's great contemporaries in the theatre, the greatest of them, Ben Jonson, had a good deal to say about Shakespeare. In his rather bibulous after-dinner conversations with William Drummond of Hawthornden in 1619 he said 'that Shakespeare wanted art', and mocked at the sea-coast which Shakespeare had attributed to Bohemia in *The Winter's Tale*:

> Shakespeare in a play brought in a number of men saying they had suffered shipwreck in Bohemia, where there is no sea near by some hundred miles.

But when he came to write his splendid poem prefixed to the Folio of 1623, Ben Jonson rose to the occasion with stirring words of praise:

> Triumph, my Britain, thou hast one to show
>   To whom all scenes of Europe homage owe,
> He was not of an age, but for all time!

The Workes of William Shakespeare,

containing all his Comedies, Histories, and
Tragedies: Truely set forth, according to their first
ORIGINALL.

The Names of the Principall Actors
in all these Playes.

William Shakespeare.

Richard Burbadge.

John Hemmings.

Augustine Phillips.

William Kempt.

Thomas Poope.

George Bryan.

Henry Condell.

William Slye.

Richard Cowly.

John Lowine.

Samuell Crosse.

Alexander Cooke.

Samuel Gilburne.

Robert Armin.

William Ostler.

Nathan Field.

John Underwood.

Nicholas Tooley.

William Ecclestone.

Joseph Taylor.

Robert Benfield.

Robert Goughe.

Richard Robinson.

Iohn Shancke.

Iohn Rice.

The Actors' List from the First Folio (1623)

And Jonson almost retracted his earlier jibe about Shakespeare's lacking art:

> Yet must I not give Nature all; thy Art,
>   My gentle Shakespeare, must enjoy a part.
> For though the poet's matter Nature be,
>   His Art doth give the fashion. And that he
> Who casts to write a living line must sweat
>   (Such as thine are) and strike the second heat
> Upon the Muse's anvil; turn the same
>   – And himself with it – that he thinks to frame;
> Or for the laurel he may gain a scorn.
>   For a good poet's made, as well as born.
> And such wert thou.

Ben Jonson gives his testimony that Shakespeare's personality was to be felt, by those who knew him, in his poetry
– that, in fact, the style was the man:

> Look how the father's face
> Lives in his issue. Even so, the race
> Of Shakespeare's mind and manners brightly shines
> In his well-turnèd and true filèd lines.

And Jonson reminds his readers of the strong impressions
that the plays of William Shakespeare of Stratford-upon-
Avon made upon Queen Elizabeth I and King James I at
Court performances:

> Sweet Swan of Avon! what a sight it were
>   To see thee in our waters yet appear,
> And make those flights upon the banks of Thames
>   That so did take Eliza and our James!

Shakespeare seems to have been on affectionate terms with
his colleagues in the theatrical enterprise with which he was
associated all his life. In his will in 1616 he bequeathed 'to
my fellows, John Heminges, Richard Burbage, and Henry
Condell, twenty six shillings and eightpence apiece to buy
them rings'. It was Heminges and Condell who dedicated

the Folio of 1623 to the Earl of Pembroke and the Earl of Montgomery, explaining that they had collected together the plays 'without ambition either of self-profit or fame; only to keep the memory of so worthy a friend and fellow alive as was our Shakespeare'. As they informed 'the great variety of readers',

It had been a thing, we confess, worthy to have been wished, that the author himself had lived to have set forth and overseen his own writings. But since it hath been ordained otherwise and he by death departed from that right, we pray you do not envy his friends the office of their care and pain, to have collected and published them.

Shakespeare's life-long colleagues knew their man and thought they understood his genius. Shakespeare was a writer,

whom, as he was a happy imitator of nature, was a most gentle expresser of it. His mind and hand went together; and what he thought, he uttered with that easiness that we have scarce received from him a blot in his papers.

Ben Jonson, himself a laborious and painstaking writer, was provoked by this praise of Shakespeare's facility and in later years wrote in his note-book:

I remember the players have often mentioned it as an honour to Shakespeare that in his writing, whatsoever he penned, he never blotted out line. My answer hath been: 'Would he had blotted a thousand'; which they thought a malevolent speech. I had not told posterity this, but for their ignorance who choose that circumstance to commend their friend by wherein he most faulted; and to justify mine own candour. For I loved the man and do honour his memory, on this side idolatry, as much as any. He was, indeed, honest, and of an open and free nature; had an excellent fancy, brave notions, and gentle expressions; wherein he flowed with that facility that sometime it was necessary he should be stopped.

Ben Jonson's bold praises of Shakespeare are not impaired by an occasional grudging attitude to the copious creativity of the greater man's genius. The 'open and free nature' seems to be confirmed, or at least not disproved, in an interesting private letter addressed to Shakespeare on 25 October 1598, and preserved in the borough archives of Stratford-upon-Avon. (It is remarkable luck that a private letter of this kind should have survived.) Richard Quiney addressed the letter from the Bell Inn in Carter Lane, London, where he had come from Stratford upon business, 'To my loving good friend and countryman, Mr Wm. Shakespeare, deliver these'. Quiney thought his fellow Stratfordian a fit person to apply to for a loan of the large sum of £30.

Loving countryman,

I am bold of you as of a friend, craving your help with £30 upon Mr Bushell's and my security, or Mr Mytton's with me. Mr Rosswell is not come to London as yet, and I have especial cause. You shall friend me much in helping me out of all the debts I owe in London, I thank God, and much quiet my mind which would not be indebted. I am now towards the Court in hope of answer for the dispatch of my business. You shall neither lose credit nor money by me, the Lord willing; and now but persuade yourself so as I hope, and you shall not need to fear but with all hearty thankfulness I will hold my time and content your friend; and if we bargain farther you shall be the paymaster yourself. My time bids me hasten to an end, and so I commit this to your care and hope of your help. I fear I shall not be back this night from the Court. Haste. The Lord be with you and with us all. Amen. From the Bell in Carter Lane, the 25 October 1598.

Yours in all kindness,
Richard Quiney

We do not know much about Quiney's business at Court, nor why he was in difficulties, nor whether he succeeded in borrowing the money from Shakespeare, nor even whether he actually sent the letter. But eighteen years later his son Thomas married Judith, Shakespeare's second daughter.

Shakespeare died on 23 April 1616, and as the part owner of the tithes he was buried in the chancel of the parish church of Stratford-upon-Avon. No name was inscribed on the gravestone; but instead the famous lines appeared (Plate 9b) of which the purpose was apparently to ensure that the body was left in peace and to prevent the moving of the bones to the adjacent charnel house. We cannot tell who wrote them. The tradition that they are Shakespeare's own goes back to the seventeenth century. It is quite possible that he was the author, for (as we know from his plays) Shakespeare had wonderful skill in composing bad or feeble poems which were perfectly appropriate for the circumstances (compare Orlando's or Hamlet's or Benedick's). Gravestone doggerel was an accepted kind of verse. A similar epitaph for a baker is known:

> For Jesus Christ his sake forbear
> To dig the bones under this bier.
> Blessèd is he who loves my dust;
> But damned be he who moves my crust.

Shakespeare's family or friends, however, were not content with a simple gravestone and within a few years a monument was erected on the chancel wall (Plate 9a). It seems to have existed by 1623, for it is referred to in a poem, prefixed to the Folio edition of Shakespeare's plays, by Leonard Digges of University College, Oxford.

> Shakespeare, at length thy pious fellows give
> The world thy *Works*; thy *Works* by which out-live
> Thy tomb thy name must. When that stone is rent,
> And time dissolves thy Stratford monument,
> Here we alive shall view thee still. This book,
> When brass and marble fade, shall make thee look
> Fresh to all ages.

The Latin epitaph on the monument, immediately under-
neath the bust, attributes to Shakespeare the wisdom of
Nestor, the genius of Socrates, and the poetic art of Virgil
(*Iudicio Pylium, genio Socratem, arte Maronem*). This
apparently was how his contemporaries at Stratford-upon-
Avon wished their fellow-citizen to be remembered.

SHAKESPEARE:
TEXTS AND CRITICISM

Kenneth Muir

ODERN editions of Shakespeare's works
are based ultimately on the cheap quarto
editions published between 1593 and
1622, and on the collected edition of
thirty-six of his plays published in 1623,
seven years after his death, known as the
First Folio. The quartos are of six different kinds:

(1) The two narrative poems, *Venus and Adonis* (1593)
and *The Rape of Lucrece* (1594), were published by Richard
Field (who came from Stratford) and they were printed
with great care from Shakespeare's own manuscripts, with
dedications to the Earl of Southampton (see page 34).

(2) *The Passionate Pilgrim* (1600), though ascribed to
Shakespeare by Jaggard, the publisher, and though it contains bad texts of three poems from *Love's Labour's Lost*
and of two of the sonnets, is filled out with poems by Marlowe, Barnfield, and others.

(3) The *Sonnets* (1609), although probably published without Shakespeare's knowledge or consent, seem to have been
printed from the poet's manuscript, or from a fairly accurate
copy of it.

(4) Seven of the plays appeared in 'bad' quartos – piratical

publications of versions obtained surreptitiously. Some of them seem to have been compiled from memory by actors on tour, and to have been sold to raise money when they were in financial straits or when the companies were reorganized. Of this kind are *The Contention betwixt the two famous Houses of York and Lancaster* (1594) and *The True Tragedy of Richard, Duke of York* (1596), debased versions of the second and third parts of *Henry VI* and not (as used to be thought) their sources. Some parts of the bad quarto of *Hamlet* (1603) are accurately reported, and from this it has been deduced that the actor who played Marcellus and Voltimand was the pirate. He eked out his memories of Shakespeare's play with echoes from an earlier play on the same subject. *Romeo and Juliet*, *The Merry Wives of Windsor* (for which the actor who played the Host of the Garter Inn was the pirate; see page 56), *Henry V*, and *Pericles* were also pirated; and there may also have been a pirated edition of *Love's Labour's Lost* of which no copies have survived.

(5) Two plays, *Richard III* and *King Lear*, appeared in what have been termed 'doubtful' quartos: they are too accurate to have been derived by the use of shorthand in the theatre, and not accurate enough to have been printed from an authentic manuscript. Some have supposed that *King Lear* was taken down from dictation by the whole company; but this theory is not generally accepted.

(6) Twelve plays appeared in good quartos, printed either from Shakespeare's 'foul papers' (i.e. not rough drafts, but the manuscript from which the prompt-copy was made) or from a copy of the manuscript. These were *Titus Andronicus* (1594), *Richard II* (1597), *Love's Labour's Lost* (1598), *Romeo and Juliet* (1599), *1* and *2 Henry IV* (1598, 1600), *The Merchant of Venice* (1600), *A Midsummer-Night's Dream* (1600), *Much Ado about Nothing* (1600), *Hamlet* (1604; see page 57), *Troilus and Cressida* (1609), and

A
Moſt pleaſaunt and
excellent conceited Co-
medie, of Syr *Iohn Falſtaffe*, and the
merrie Wiues of *Windſor*.

Entermixed with ſundrie
variable and pleaſing humors, of Syr *Hugh*
the Welch Knight, Iuſtice *Shallow*, and his
wiſe Couſin M. *Slender*.

With the ſwaggering vaine of Auncient
Piſtoll, and Corporall *Nym*.

By *William Shakeſpeare*.

As it hath bene diuers times Acted by the right Honorable
my Lord Chamberlaines ſeruants. Both before her
Maieſtie, and elſe-where.

LONDON
Printed by **T. C.** for Arthur Iohnſon, and are to be ſold at
his ſhop in Powles Church-yard, at the ſigne of the
Flower de Leuſe and the Crowne.
1602.

Title-page of the 'Bad' Quarto of *The Merry Wiues of Windſor*, 1602

THE
Tragicall Hiſtorie of
HAMLET,

Prince of Denmarke.

By William Shakeſpeare.

Newly imprinted and enlarged to almoſt as much
againe as it was, according to the true and perfect
Coppie.

AT LONDON,
Printed by I. R. for N. L. and are to be ſold at his
ſhoppe vnder Saint Dunſtons Church in
Fleetſtreet. 1 6 0 5.

Title-page of the 'Good' Quarto of *Hamlet*, 1604–5.

Othello (1622) – though not every editor regards this last as
a good quarto. Two or three of the twelve were probably
released by the actors to replace bad quartos. The plays be-
longed not to the author but to the company of actors, who
naturally preferred not to publish the plays while they were
still in their repertory. They probably sold some of the plays
at times when the theatres were closed on account of the
plague. There is no evidence that Shakespeare corrected the
proofs of any of his plays and even the good quartos were
carelessly printed. Since proofs were corrected during the
actual printing and the uncorrected sheets were bound up
with corrected sheets, individual copies of the same edition
differ from each other. *King Lear*, the extreme case, has
167 variants in the first edition; and sometimes the uncorrected reading, although nonsense, is nearer to what Shakespeare wrote than the wrongly 'corrected' reading. Many of
the quartos were reprinted several times, and each new
edition, while correcting some obvious mistakes, introduced
many additional errors. The first good quarto, therefore, is
always more reliable than later reprints.

The First Folio was edited by Shakespeare's fellow-actors,
John Heminges and Henry Condell. They excluded plays
which had been wrongly attributed to Shakespeare. They
also excluded *Pericles* (of which no accurate text was available, and the first two acts of which Shakespeare merely
revised) and *The Two Noble Kinsmen* (written by Shakespeare in collaboration with John Fletcher); but they included the first part of *Henry VI*, which some critics have
believed to be a composite work, and also *Timon of Athens*
which cannot have been performed in the text as published.
The copy they used was of various kinds. Some plays were
printed from good quartos which had either been used as
prompt copies, or had been corrected by comparison with
the prompt-book. They normally used the latest available
quarto, and they did not eliminate all the errors which had

been introduced into the text since the publication of the first edition. Other plays, which had not been published before, were printed from the prompt-book or from scribal copies.

During the years that had elapsed since the plays were first performed, alterations had been made in the text, for most of which Shakespeare was not responsible. Cuts were made, either for Court performances or to shorten plays which were thought to be excessively long. Among the cuts made in the Folio edition of *Hamlet* was the whole of the hero's last sililoquy ('How all occasions do inform against me'). Equally damaging were the alterations made by the actors. They added, for example, the Hecate scene in *Macbeth*; they substituted *bitter* for *acerbe* in Iago's part; they added 'O, O, O, O, O' to Hamlet's last words, 'The rest is silence'. Sometimes they corrected faulty metre. Faced with the line (in the 1622 quarto of *Richard III*)

That tempts him to this extremity

they inserted 'harsh' before the last word; but we know from the first quarto that Shakespeare actually wrote

That tempers him to this extremity.

Also many oaths were removed from the text bacause of an Act against blasphemy. In the letter read by Malvolio, and in his later exclamation 'Jove be thanked', 'Jove' may be a substitution for 'God'.

But the actual printing of the Folio was much more careful than that of any of the quartos, and not merely better than that of the 'divers stolen and surreptitious copies, maimed and deformed by the frauds and stealths of injurious impostors' to which Heminges and Condell referred. Nevertheless, for the reasons given, a modern editor will base his text on the good quartos where available (except possibly *Troilus and Cressida* and *Othello*) and he will accept Folio readings only when they are necessary corrections, and not merely 'sophistications', as the Folio's illegitimate alterations are called.

Three other Folios were published during the seventeenth century, and each of them corrected some mistakes and introduced others. Nicholas Rowe's edition (1709) was followed during the next two hundred years by many others. Editors added stage directions and also the location of scenes – a convenience to readers which perpetuated wrong ideas about the Elizabethan stage. Although some of the earlier editors realized the importance of the quartos, they all based their texts on the Folios. Pope (1725) omitted some passages from his text and they were (to use his own words) 'degraded to the bottom of the page', because he believed them to be interpolations by the actors; and he smoothed out Shakespeare's metrical irregularities. But modern readers owe a great debt to the line of eighteenth-century editors, not merely for their explanatory notes, but for their improvement of the text.

Some of their emendations we, with our greater knowledge of Elizabethan vocabulary and idiom, now know to have been unnecessary; others have been superseded; but a large number have been almost universally accepted – for example, Theobald's emendation of 'a Table of greene fields' in the account of Falstaff's death to 'a' babbled of green fields'. Of the emendations generally accepted into the text of (for example) *Richard II*, Rowe, Theobald, Hanmer, and Johnson suggested one apiece, Pope and Malone two apiece, and Capell three.

By 1864, the three-hundredth anniversary of Shakespeare's birth, the textual work of eighteenth- and nineteenth-century editors was embodied in the great Cambridge edition and in its one-volume offspring, the Globe Shakespeare, which became for many people the standard text. But in the present century the science of bibliography has made great strides.

The relationship of the Folio to the Quartos has been determined with some degree of unanimity; the habits of compositors have been examined and even their relative competence; and it is now generally accepted that three pages of *Sir Thomas More* are in Shakespeare's own handwriting, a study of which has thrown some light on possible misreadings by compositors. Sir Walter Greg's *The Editorial Problem in Shakespeare* (1942; 2nd edition, 1951) and *The Shakespeare First Folio* (1955) provided authoritative statements of textual orthodoxy at the time they were written; but they need to be considered alongside Alice Walker's *Textual Problems of the First Folio* (1953) and the numerous writings of Fredson Bowers and his bibliographical school. The new bibliography has led to greater reliance on the good quartos and to some valuable emendations. If one compares the one-volume editions of Peter Alexander and C. J. Sisson with the Globe, or the New Cambridge with the old, or the New Arden with the old, one must be struck by the cumulative effect of hundreds of small changes. Recent volumes in the New Variorum Shakespeare, compared with those which appeared in the nineteenth century, exhibit the same textual revolution.

These volumes also exhibit the present impossibility of summarizing in one volume all that has been said about any of the major plays. For the gradual establishment of what Shakespeare wrote — a process, however, which will never be complete — has been accompanied by a huge proliferation of criticism and interpretation, beginning with stray remarks made by Shakespeare's contemporaries and the great elegy which Ben Jonson wrote for the First Folio, and ending with the publication every year of hundreds of books and articles. The change, even during the past century, can be illustrated by the case of a minor play. A hundred years ago, not a single good article had been published on *Love's Labour's Lost*; now, an adequate bibliography of the play would contain the titles of several books, chapters from scores of others, and perhaps fifty articles. The process began slowly, but it accelerates every year. During the period of the Restoration, the only valuable criticism of Shakespeare was by Dryden. The eighteenth-century editors provided introductory essays on Shakespeare's work, Johnson especially rising above the prejudices of his time to give a wonderfully phrased eulogy of his genius. The second half of the century, the period which saw what has been called the genesis of 'Shakespeare idolatry', is notable for the famous essay by Maurice Morgann and for the first study of Shakespeare's imagery in Walter Whiter's *A Specimen of a Commentary*. In the Romantic period, Coleridge in his lectures concentrated, although not exclusively, on the characters of Shakespeare's plays – this was the title of Hazlitt's book. This kind of criticism culminated in A. C. Bradley's *Shakespearean Tragedy* (1903). Meanwhile a great deal of information had been collected during the nineteenth century about Shakespeare's life and reading, his contemporaries, his stage, even his birds and flowers, but there was a singular dearth of first-rate criticism. Three essays by Walter Pater have worn better than the once standard books of Brandes and Gervinus; and we are out of sympathy with Dowden's influential *Shakspere, His Mind and Art* because it presupposes too close a relationship between Shakespeare's life and works, with Moulton's *Shakespeare as a Dramatic Artist* because it seems to impose on the plays an inorganic rather than an organic unity, and with Swinburne's books because of their inflated style.

In the present century, the output of Shakespeare scholarship and criticism is so enormous that it is impossible to do more than refer to some of the more important books. The facts about Shakespeare's life and work had no sooner been assembled in Sir Edmund Chambers's *William Shakespeare: Facts and Problems* than Leslie Hotson provided some additional information about the poet's quarrel with Justice Gardiner and about his Stratford friends in *Shakespeare Versus Shallow* and *I, William Shakespeare*. T. W. Baldwin has written two learned volumes on the curricula of the primary and secondary schools of Shakespeare's day, and other books on the 'literary genetics' of his early poems and plays. These are splendid repositories of information, although Baldwin's deductions from it are often questionable. Geoffrey Bullough has collected, with judicious introductions, the *Narrative and Dramatic Sources* of Shakespeare, V. K. Whitaker has written admirably on *Shakespeare's Use of Learning*, J. A. K. Thomson on *Shakespeare and the Classics,* and Richmond Noble on *Shakespeare's Knowledge of the Bible.* There have been many other books and articles on Shakespeare's reading, but a comprehensive study, to supersede Anders's *Shakespeare's Books,* is still to be written. The received ideas of Shakespeare's day have been studied in E. M. W. Tillyard's *The Elizabethan World Picture* and Hardin Craig's *The Enchanted Glass.*

Our knowledge of Shakespeare's stage and audience has been extended by such books as G. Kernodle's *From Art to Theatre*, C. Walter Hodges's *The Globe Restored,* Glynne Wickham's *Early English Stages,* Muriel C. Bradbrook's *The Rise of the Common Player,* B. L. Joseph's *Elizabethan Acting,* and Alfred Harbage's *Shakespeare's Audience, As They Liked It,* and *The Rival Traditions.* Leslie Hotson, in his controversial books *The First Night of 'Twelfth Night'* and *Shakespeare's Wooden O* has argued that the audience sat all round the stage, and not merely on three sides of it. The debate continues on this subject, some critics arguing that there was no room for the groundlings to stand at the side of the stage. The influence of stage conditions and conventions on Shakespeare's plays has been studied in E. E. Stoll's numerous books, the best being *Art and Artifice in Shakespeare*; his main point is that Shakespeare's characters are theatrically, but not psychologically, convincing. This was a natural reaction against the character-criticism which culminated in Bradley's masterpiece. L. Schücking stressed the survival of primitive techniques in Elizabethan drama – the direct addressing of the audience, the use of choric characters, the sacrifice of consistency of characterization to immediate theatrical effect – but not all have agreed that such techniques were primitive as used by Shakespeare. Stoll and Schücking were attacked by J. I. M. Stewart in his *Character and Motive in Shakespeare* and he sought to show that the behaviour of characters could be justified by a more modern psychology than that used by Stoll. Muriel C. Bradbrook in *Elizabethan Stage Conventions* and *Elizabethan Tragedy* and S. L. Bethell in *Shakespeare and the Popular Dramatic Tradition* have discussed the conventions in a more positive way.

Among books on style and language, Sister Miriam Joseph's *Shakespeare's Use of the Arts of Language* is a valuable introduction to Renaissance rhetoric and to its use by Shakespeare. It may be supplemented by M. M. Mahood's *Shakespeare's Word-Play*. The function of imagery has been studied in Caroline Spurgeon's *Shakespeare's Imagery* and, with greater dramatic understanding, by W. H. Clemen in *The Development of Shakespeare's Imagery*. More recently, Maurice Charney has written on the imagery of the Roman plays; and R. B. Heilman has written two full-length books on the imagery of *King Lear* and *Othello: This Great Stage* and *Magic in the Web*. G. Wilson Knight makes use of imagery and symbolism in his interpretations of the plays from *The Wheel of Fire* to *The Sovereign Flower* and his approach has made him one of the most influential, but most controversial, interpreters of Shakespeare.

Numerous books, published during the present century, have attempted either to give a comprehensive idea of Shakespeare's works, or at least to deal with one aspect of them

Of general surveys may be mentioned those by Sir Walter Raleigh, J. Middleton Murry, Mark van Doren, Peter Alexander, H. S. Goddard, and H. Fluchère; of studies of particular aspects Theodore Spencer's *Shakespeare and the Nature of Man*, Arthur Sewell's *Character and Society in Shakespeare*, D. G. James's *The Dream of Learning*, W. C. Curry's *Shakespeare's Philosophical Patterns*, A. P. Rossiter's *Angel with Horns*, and L. C. Knights's *Some Shakespearean Themes* are among the most notable.

Many critics have concentrated on a single group of Shakespeare's plays. On the Histories there have been valuable books by Lily B. Campbell, E. M. W. Tillyard, M. M. Reese, and Derek Traversi, in addition to *The Fortunes of Falstaff* by J. Dover Wilson. The best books on the comedies are probably those of J. R. Brown, C. L. Barber, and Bertrand Evans, although those of Dover Wilson, T. M. Parrott, E. C. Pettet, and H. B. Charlton have their admirers. Tillyard and W. W. Lawrence have written on the problem plays, and under this category E. Schanzer includes *Julius Caesar* and *Antony and Cleopatra*, but not *All's Well that Ends Well* and *Troilus and Cressida*. Dozens of books have been written on the tragedies during the past sixty years, of which those by Lily B. Campbell, H. S. Wilson, John Lawlor, John Holloway, Irving Ribner, and Willard Farnham are representative of different approaches. M. W. MacCallum's is still the standard book on the Roman plays. Tillyard, Traversi, and G. Wilson Knight have written books on the plays of the last period.

Some books deal with individual plays and among these should be mentioned Frances M. Yates on *Love's Labour's Lost*, Leslie Hotson and J. W. Draper on *Twelfth Night*, Mary Lascelles on *Measure for Measure*; J. Dover Wilson, Peter Alexander, Roy Walker, G. R. Elliot, B. L. Joseph, H. Levin, and L. C. Knights on *Hamlet*; G. R. Elliott and B. Spivack on *Othello*; J. F. Danby and R. A. Fraser on

King Lear; and Roy Walker and H. N. Paul on *Macbeth*. Edward Hubler has written an admirable book on the *Sonnets*. H. Granville-Barker's *Prefaces* to many of the plays, several of them book-length, contain some excellent advice on how the plays should be produced and how the characters should be played.

It should be emphasized, however, that some of the best criticism of Shakespeare's plays is to be found in uncollected essays, in introductions to individual plays, and scattered through the dramatic criticisms of Bernard Shaw, iconoclast though he was.

It is difficult for the general reader to know what to read, and what not to read – for some of the least reliable books have had the largest sales. The standard bibliography and the standard history of Shakespeare criticism are both out of date; but the nine booklets on Shakespeare in the 'Writers and their Work' series (published for the British Council and the National Book League by Longmans) contain reasonably full lists of books and articles. The latest developments of scholarship and criticism can be followed in *Shakespeare Survey* (published annually) and in the American *Shakespeare Quarterly*.

At Stratford-upon-Avon the libraries of the Shakespeare Birthplace Trust and the Royal Shakespeare Theatre are being amalgamated in the new Shakespeare Centre in 1964, and here also the University of Birmingham maintains the Shakespeare Institute. Apart from the great libraries at Oxford, Cambridge, London, and Edinburgh, the best English Shakespeare collection is to be found in the Birmingham Public Library; but it is far surpassed by the splendid Folger Shakespeare Library in Washington, D.C., which has an unrivalled collection of books by Shakespeare and his contemporaries.

SHAKESPEARE
AND THE ACTORS

John Russell Brown

HILE the world pays homage to Shakespeare, actors may spend what time they have in returning thanks. He was abundantly generous to actors, giving them opportunities to shine in large parts and small, to use invention and imagination, voice, body, musical sense, intelligence, their whole personalities. Some dramatists leave little for actors to do; they must speak their text and fill positions in a dramatic pattern. Others have become successful by leaving almost everything for the actors to create. Shakespeare stands between these, not in any compromising way, but by writing magniloquent roles and splendid scenes, by giving every kind of help that a dramatist can, and at the same time allowing his interpreters all the scope they could desire for their own contribution to the play in performance. Shakespearian actors can feel sustained and free.

By reading a text anyone can understand how much Shakespeare gives: words, themes, plots, characters, fantasy, ceremony, reality, in a total impression and in short phrases that seem to leap into the mind from the printed page and stay and develop or change there. But his invitation to the actor to give is more of a secret; it is revealed gradually during rehearsals and always retains some element of mystery. It seems to be addressed individually to each actor, and only its broadest proffers are common knowledge. There is the opportunity to suggest behind the main business of early scenes the inner man who is to be revealed at the conclusion, to show behind the quick dignity and irreverence of Richard II in his time of power the doomed prisoner who hammers out his fate, wins the 'heart' of his groom, and unarmed kills two of his assailants. Each actor can discover these opportunities according to his own talents and personality but, if the play is to live in performance fully, he must make his full contribution. A Coriolanus must know how he can stand silent, and turn away from his mother, so that her long speech is truly a duologue and at the end the audience will watch a small movement: '*He holds her by the hand, silent*', and be satisfied that his decision has been made, and with a deep consciousness of what it implies. A Feste must find means to reconcile the several aspects of his part: the professional fool who jests for money, the instinctive impersonator, the barren fool, the sentimental fool, and the wise. His last riddling song must be a full conclusion to the comedy answering all the expectations which that particular performance has awakened in the audience. The actor cannot leave this effect to Shakespeare or to the composer of the music; the audience will be attentive to the newly emptied stage, and the new quietness; it will respond to his smallest movement or change of tempo or pitch or inflexion: he has been given the play to hold.

There are corporate opportunities too: the wonder and resistance of the last scene of *The Tempest*, the uneasy watchfulness in the Court of Elsinore, the precarious and individual delight of each lover and actor at the end of *A Midsummer Night's Dream*. These are large invitations, the obvious encouragements which quicken the hopes and genius of every actor.

Whether the Chamberlain's Men (later to become the King's Men) developed this generosity in Shakespeare, or whether his way of writing affected the composition of his actors' company, we shall never know. But, certainly, he stayed with the one set of 'fellows' all his career, and shared with them the ownership of theatres and the profits of productions; he acted with them as late as 1603. It is not surprising that their company seems to have been well adapted to his plays. It could depend upon the *ensemble* performance that only a permanent group can give, but it also had its star performers. Actors made the competent fortunes from the Elizabethan theatres, rather than the dramatists. Burbage (Plate 16a), Lowin, Tarlton, and Kemp were widely known and had their equivalents of fans: as Hamlet welcomes his 'old friend' among the 'Tragedians of the City', so Richard Burbage was the 'old acquaintance' of the Earl of Pembroke. One dramatist likened the hero of his tragedy, *Barnavelt*, to a leading player:

with such murmurs as glad spectators in a theatre grace their best actors with, they ever heard him, when to have had a sight of him, was held a prosperous omen; when no eye gazed on him that was not filled with admiration.

Burbage earned a reputation for never making an exit 'but with applause' and Shakespeare, as an actor who did not become a star, would have had good occasion for knowing that:

> in a theatre, the eyes of men,
> After a well-graced actor leaves the stage,
> Are idly bent on him that enters next,
> Thinking his prattle to be tedious.

The star actors gained in reputation and power during Shakespeare's career, but from the first the company seems to have been able to achieve the quick cooperation necessary for gusty battle-scenes and for the neat and complicated interplay of *The Comedy of Errors* and *The Taming of the Shrew*. Of course there were difficulties: clowns so famed as personality performers that they were likely to say more than was 'set down for them', supernumeraries who could turn a battle into a 'brawl ridiculous'. But Shakespeare continued to write battle-scenes and to give his clowns 'fat' parts.

Hamlet complains of the actor who speaks his lines like a town-crier; and Ulysses describes the

> strutting player, whose conceit
> Lies in his hamstring, and doth think it rich
> To hear the wooden dialogue and sound
> 'Twixt his stretch'd footing and the scaffoldage.

But at their best Elizabethan actors could respond to the artifice of Shakespeare's poetry and, at the same time, 'imitate Nature'. Rhetorical delivery that gave considered clarity to tropes and figures of speech, and suited 'the action to the word, the word to the action', was taught in every grammar-school, so that when Polonius praises a rendering of a speech from a play for 'good accent and good discretion' he was assessing a common skill in common terms. But while a book of *Characters* (1615) said of 'An Excellent Actor' that 'whatsoever is commendable in the grave orator is most exquisitely perfect in him', it also testified that

what we see him personate, we think truly done before us: a man of a deep thought might apprehend the ghosts of our ancient heroes walked again, and take him (at several times) for many of them.

Burbage could act a death-scene so realistically that it was said that even the actors on stage with him sometimes thought that he had actually died. Spectators were known to have jumped on to the stage to save their hero from what appeared to be a real blow. Shakespeare's actors were trained

to respond to all the musical, formal, and imaginative qualities of his speeches, and to all their realism – their 'imitation
of life', as an Elizabethan would say.

In two ways the Elizabethan actors baffle our understanding: the size of their repertories and the use of boys for
women's parts.

During 1594 and 1595 one of several rival companies performed thirty new plays, and if one received twelve or fifteen
unconsecutive performances during that time it would rank
as a respectable success. We have no list of plays produced
by the Chamberlain's or King's Men during any one year,
but we do know that in the spring of 1613 they were paid for
'fourteen several plays' performed as part of the celebrations
for a royal wedding. Some were old pieces, like *Much Ado
About Nothing*, first performed a dozen or so years before;
and this may be a clue to the maintenance of a large repertory
with high standards of acting: if a play proved accept-
able the same cast would work together on it for many
seasons.

The skill of Elizabethan boy-actors we shall never understand, for the conditions in which they worked cannot be
reproduced: the absence of actresses for comparison, the
rhetorical training in schools, the system of apprenticeship
to senior actors, the playing of female parts in one company
for as long as eight years, and the slow graduation to the
heroines. But in trying to reconstruct early performances we
should remember that contemporary accounts of their acting
in adult companies make no concessions; Cleopatra's jibe at
the 'squeaking' boy is a special case. They aimed, like their
elders, at an 'imitation of life'. In Jonson's *The Devil is an
Ass* (1616) a story is told of Dick Robinson masquerading in
real life as a lawyer's wife:

> to see him behave it;
> And lay the law; and carve; and drink unto 'em;
> And then talk bawdy: and send frolics! O!

This boy-actor could pass stage-tricks for true coin. They were helped, of course, by their dramatists, and in this Shakespeare was particularly careful. Many small roles, like Phoebe or Audrey in *As You Like It* or Octavia in *Antony and Cleopatra*, derive much of their effect from the contrasts, sequences, and rhythms of a whole play. More obviously demanding roles, like Ophelia, are often given few appearances, and some of those with secondary characters, or for a solo-like scene that could be intensively rehearsed on its own; Ophelia is alone with Hamlet only once, and the same is true of Gertrude. A Rosalind has to sustain long scenes but she is given speeches so witty and energetic that the audience has no leisure for idle inquisition, and when near the close she has to show 'strange powers' Shakespeare allowed her to be self-consciously theatrical and contrived an echoing and contrasting chorus on stage; for her reappearance in female clothes he brought on three other couples so that her happiness with Orlando is supported and defined by others' and seen as part of a full stage-picture. Shakespeare accepted the limitations of boy-actors without confining his imagination, for future generations of actresses have not found it difficult to accept their roles; they may cut or underplay some of the verbal wit and refuse some of the restrictions of the text, but still there has been enough in Shakespeare's plays to awaken both their full talents and their imaginations.

The history of Shakespearian acting since the first days to the four-hundredth anniversary of his birth is partly an account of textual additions, omissions, and adaptations. This was inevitable as each age approached his plays with different predispositions and offered different theatrical talents, stages, and audiences. The happy ending of Nahum Tate's *Lear* or the transvestite amusements of *The Enchanted Island* (by Dryden and Davenant) and later versions of *The Tempest* may savour of overweening presumption in

THAMESIS

13. Bankside, from Visscher's *View of London*, 1616.

MR. WILLIAM
SHAKESPEARES

COMEDIES,
HISTORIES, &
TRAGEDIES.

Published according to the True Originall Copies.

Martin Droeshout Sculpsit London.

LONDON

Printed by Isaac Iaggard, and Ed. Bl

. Martin Droeshout's engraving of Shakespeare. The earliest
own state; from a copy of the First Folio.

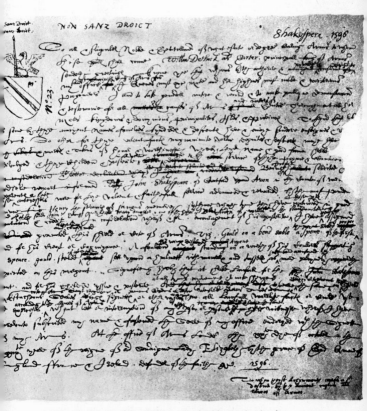

15. The first draft of Sir William Dethick's entries in the
Heralds' College as to the assignment of arms to John
Shakespeare, 1596-9.

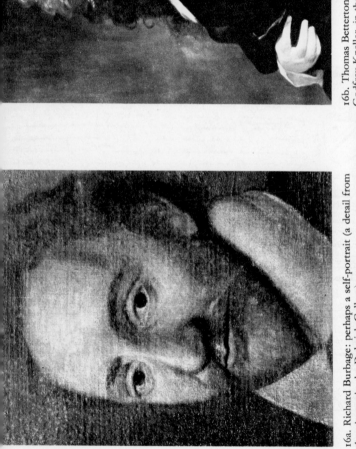

16a. Richard Burbage: perhaps a self-portrait (a detail from the picture in the Dulwich Gallery).

16b. Thomas Betterton: a painting by (or after) Sir Godfrey Kneller, in the National Portrait Gallery.

18a. Sarah Siddons as Lady Macbeth sleep-walking; by G. H. Harlow.

18b. John Philip Kemble as Coriolanus, by Sir Thomas Lawrence 1798.

19a. Edmund Kean as Richard III, by J. J. Halls, 1815.

19b. Sir Henry Irving as King Lear, by Bernard Partridge: from the Souvenir Programme, Lyceum Theatre, London, 1892.

20a. Ellen Terry as Portia in *The Merchant of Venice*: from *The Illustrated London News*, 1880

20b. The Souvenir Programme of Sir Beerbohm Tree's production of *Twelfth Night*, 1902.

adapter and actors, but time has brought its revaluations. Although there are some scenes which are still completely banished from our theatres (like the discovery and forgiveness of Aumerle in *Richard II* and Launcelot's jokes about raising the price of hogs by converting Jews to Christians in *The Merchant of Venice*), and if others (like the last scene of *King Lear*) are not performed in full, we now know that the texts remain, outlasting fashions, a mine of theatrical opportunity that can be seriously, flippantly, experimentally, innocently relied upon to awaken performances of genius, and so reveal new and old measures of their inherent wealth.

Since his own age the mutual achievements of Shakespeare and the actors have usually been individual successes. Very few companies have had the permanence and close-knit interests that are necessary for overall histrionic success; for *ensemble* performance we have substituted stylistic and interpretative unity, the contrivance of the new functionary, the director. (Can we ever come within hailing distance of the acting abilities of a company that had Shakespeare as a fellow throughout his career?) The fortunes of Shakespeare and the actors after the Restoration can be briefly told by considering the great actors of the English theatre and what they have given and discovered.

Thomas Betterton (1635–1710; see Plate 16b) brought the qualities of Restoration heroic and Court drama. Declamation, an elevated tone, and decorum, were important considerations in his theatre. Colley Cibber praised him for corresponding virtues:

Could *how* Betterton spoke be as easily known as *what* he spoke; then might you see the Muse of Shakespeare triumph, with all her beauties in their best array, rising into real life, and charming her beholders.

He combined reality with what seemed a triumphant 'beauty'. (Betterton is an early example of a fine Shakespeare actor distinguished among his contemporaries by his hold on an impression of 'real life'.) At this time Shakespeare's text seemed designed to sustain a consistent and considered impression of emotion and fine sentiment: on seeing his father's ghost, Betterton's Hamlet

opened with a pause of mute amazement; then rising slowly, to a solemn, trembling voice, he made the Ghost equally terrible to the spectator, as to himself; and in the descriptive part of the natural emotions which the ghastly vision gave him, the boldness of this expostulation was still governed by decency, manly but not braving; his voice never rising into . . . wild defiance of what he naturally revered.

So fully did Shakespeare's plays encourage assurance and simplicity of dramatic focus that this style became grossly exaggerated by Betterton's imitators. *The Rosciad* (1761) pictures an actor's entry:

> with truly tragic stalk,
> He creeps, he flies, – a hero should not walk.
> As if with heaven he warr'd his eager eyes
> Planted their batteries against the skies;
> Attitude, action, air, pause, start, sigh, groan,
> He borrow'd, and made use of as his own.

Charles Macklin (1700–97) and, still more effectively, David Garrick (1717–79; see Plate 17) rebelled against this imitative and pompous way of playing. They stressed 'familiar' elements and studied their roles unaffectedly. According to his biographer:

Mr Garrick took all the necessary steps and precautions, previous to his appearance on a London stage, to ensure his success when he should come forth a candidate for fame. He had performed a noviciate at Ipswich; and even before his going to that place, he had studied, with great assiduity, a variety of parts on the different walks of acting. The Clown, the Fop, the Fine Gentleman, the Man of Humour, the Sot, the Valet, the Lover, the Hero, nay, the Harlequin, had all been critically examined and often rehearsed and practised by him in private.

Shakespeare now seemed fit for acting that could break across established categories, and was supported by private, individual study. Garrick decided to appear first as Richard III; his

easy and familiar, yet forcible style in speaking and acting, at first threw the critics into some hesitation concerning the novelty as well as the propriety of his manner. ... To the just modulation of the words, and concurring expression of the features from the genuine workings of nature, they had been strangers, at least for some time. ... [But] when the actor, having thrown aside the hypocrite and politician, assumed the warrior and the hero ... the words:

> Off with his head!
> So much for Buckingham!

were so significant and important, from his visible enjoyment of the incident, that several loud shouts of approbation proclaimed the triumph of the actor.

(Ironically enough, the words quoted here are among the many added by Colley Cibber in his drastic but long-popular adaptation.) Garrick showed that Shakespeare's dialogue could support nervous and subtle emphasis; indeed, one of his critics said that he paid 'too close regard to the passion and meaning of the author'. The various and conflicting stresses of Hamlet's first soliloquy, for example, were revealed and accentuated:

The last of the words: 'So excellent a king' is utterly lost; it is caught only from the movement of the mouth, which quivers and shuts tight immediately afterwards, so as to restrain the all too distinct expression of grief.

Again the actor's discovery encouraged exaggerations so that in time stress could become agitation, and honest study the pursuit of singularity.

Sarah Siddons (1775–1831; Plate 18a) and John Philip Kemble (1757–1823) in different ways establish a new lofty manner. As her own account of her study of Lady Macbeth shows, Mrs Siddons looked for points of contrast and subtlety; at the hour planned for Duncan's murder, the 'daring fiend ... now enters the gallery in eager expectation', and

in the tremendous suspense of these moments ... one trait of tender feeling is expressed, 'Had he not resembled my father as he slept, I had done it.' Her humanity vanishes, however, in the same instant.

Within a portrait of a woman 'possessed' by the 'passion of ambition' and by fiends, Mrs Siddons strove to show traces of the subjugated 'charms and graces of personal beauty ..., fair, feminine, nay, perhaps, even fragile.' The result was acclaimed as Shakespeare's triumph and Mrs Siddons's; Hazlitt argued:

In speaking of the character of Lady Macbeth, we ought not to pass over Mrs Siddons's manner of acting that part. We can conceive of nothing grander. ... Power was seated on her brow, passion emanated from her breast, as from a shrine.

Loftiness, power, and passion became the acknowledged attributes of Shakespeare's tragedies. Coleridge spoke of *Antony and Cleopatra* in terms that the actors had called forth years before: he praised Shakespeare's 'insight into the nature of the passions' and the 'fiery force ... sustained throughout', with 'numerous momentary flashes of nature'.

Kemble (Plate 18b) had less passion, but more consistency. Benjamin Haydon said that he:

came into a part with a stately dignity, as if he disdained to listen to nature, however she might whisper, until he had examined and weighed the value of her counsel.

He would cut away lines or incidents that disturbed a single development of characterization and organize the stage-movement of his cast so that he was presented as the central figure of some historical painting executed according to Sir Joshua Reynolds's rules. (Like many of his contemporaries, he studied ancient statues and paintings for inspiration.) He showed to best advantage in 'those characters in which there is a predominating tinge of some over-mastering passion, or acquired habit of acting and speaking, colouring the whole man'; and this, as Sir Walter Scott saw, directed him to the 'patrician pride of Coriolanus, the stoicism of Brutus'. However unlikely this approach may seem to us, it brought Kemble to the height of his profession against strong competition: parts of Shakespeare's roles, if not a whole play, became nobly effective. The terse phrases of Coriolanus, as 'I banish you' or 'You common cry of curs', could be given the consolidated force which they need if they are to live up to their contexts. His entrances among the scattering rabble or tired soldiers were appropriate moments for a statuesque fullness:

It was impossible not to admire the noble proportions and majestic *contour* of his figure; the expression of his face ... his right arm erected in conscious authority; his chest thrown forward, and his head slightly back; his right leg fearlessly advanced, and firmness in all his attitude.

Edmund Kean (1787–1833) and William Charles Macready (1793–1873) were the 'romantic' stars of this time. Even Kean's admirers confessed that he lacked 'poetry' and 'gravity', but this was the price paid for a combined impression of passion and intellect; he was 'energetic or nothing'. Hazlitt called his appearance as Macbeth after murdering Duncan a 'heart-rending lesson of common humanity':

The hesitation, the bewildered look, the coming to himself when he sees his hands bloody; the manner in which his voice clung to his throat, and choked his utterance; his agony and tears, the force of nature overcome by passion – beggared description. It was a scene which no one who saw it can ever efface from his recollection.

Kean looked for moments of intense feeling, especially in astonishing changes of mood, or 'transitions' as his contemporaries called them: 'like thunder', his Macbeth shouted 'Hang out our banners on the outward walls' and then suddenly paused, 'dropped his double-handled sword to the ground and leaning on it, whispered, "The cry is still they come, they come"'; and with this trick he seemed 'to become ashy grey with fear.' Kean demonstrated the ability of some of Shakespeare's lines (and the stage-business they imply) to sustain performances of total, heightened involvement. A theatre-goer explained in 1816:

We were very near the stage, where I could enjoy and appreciate Kean's acting. He has the disadvantage of a small person, but with an amazing power of expression in his face. He is less noble and dignified than Kemble, but I think his genius is as great in his way. Every word he utters is full of power, and I know not whether he most excels in the terrific or in the tender and pathetic.

Richard III (Plate 19a), Shylock, Othello, and Iago were the roles he made his own.

Within this kind of striking style, Macready attempted a 'common touch': 'to express uneasiness and agitation', complained Hazlitt, 'he composes his cravat as he would in a drawing room'. He was famed for 'portraying the domestic affections' or for the 'expression of domestic tenderness' and 'noble tenderness'. He was particularly effective in *King Lear* to which he restored many lines of Shakespeare's text. As King John, having named Arthur's 'death' to Hubert, he 'started back appalled by the sense of having overleaped all safety', and looked in terror, 'in agony of suspense', to know what effect it had. From Macready to later Victorian actors the development was straight. In Henry Irving (1838–1905) the search for detailed enactment led to a controlled picturesque style given strength by solemn emotion and a consistency that refused to devise sudden thrilling moments, or 'points' as they were then called. Hamlet, Shylock, and, although it suffered from a disastrous first-night, King Lear (Plate 19b), seem to have called forth Irving's greatest gifts. His stage-business was original and inventive, though too often anti-poetic. Shaw said that his Lear failed because he tried to interpolate 'a most singular and fantastic notion of an old man'. On 'The play's the thing With which I'll catch the conscience of the king' his prompt-book of *Hamlet* noted: 'Ring down sharp as Mr Irving places his tablets against the pillar (up RC) to write'; one of his audience described the effect:

With an exuberance exactly corresponding in another groove of feeling with the quasi-hysterical use of his tablets in the First Act, he rushes to a pillar, and, placing his notebook against it, begins, as the Act-drop descends, to scribble hints for the speech he means to write.

Now Shakespeare had become the creator of 'human' characters who is praised in the literary criticism of the turn of the century; supported by Irving, by Archer's praise of Ibsen, and by concepts of characterization from late Victorian novels, the actors found that they had been provided with a crowded gallery of portraits. The comedies were in favour. Beerbohm Tree (1853–1917) gave them sumptuous settings and created a Malvolio that became an accepted 'reading': 'Mr Tree,' said the *Daily Telegraph*,

turns him into an extravagant 'elegant', a 'superior person' . . . , a puffed-up, conceited, inexpressibly self-satisfied gallant, with an ineffable condescension for lesser beings and an affable and benign toleration of Jupiter himself . . . An extravagant and highly coloured impersonation truly, not unsuggestive of the Lord Chamberlains of comic opera, and with a retinue of faithful and mirthful attendants, who precede or follow him after the manner of a pantomime baron's retainers, blithe and gay.

Malvolio and four of his attendants fill the decorative cover of the Souvenir Programme from Her Majesty's Theatre (Plate 20b). Ellen Terry portrayed what she called in lectures 'The Triumphant Women' and 'The Pathetic Women' of Shakespeare's plays; as Portia (Plate 20a), when Bassanio chose the right casket, she allowed the rose she had been holding between her hands to fall broken into an urn, and she then stooped to savour its sweetness.

It would be wrong to suggest that the actors at the turn of last century were always adding to Shakespeare. Ellen Terry and Irving have both left records of their long study of the texts and their testing of lines, turning them many ways before they were satisfied. The American actor, Richard Mansfield (1857–1907), in an interview to *The New York Herald* in 1902 about his interpretation of Brutus, exemplifies the kind of attention they brought to the text. He said that Brutus:

was a dreamer of great things, just as he was a doer of dire things, for noble ends; but sundry hints are in the part of a wordly sense that is at seeming variance with pure idealism ... Did he not see that the thought of the intolerable in Julius Caesar's attitude was brought before him to stimulate an ambition in Brutus himself as the man to succeed Caesar? He knew what Cassius was driving at, and let it somewhat tempt him ... It is curious how notes in this direction occur in the orchard episodes for those who seek them. ... But these were minor shadings of the character and had to fall in subordinate to the broader conception of him as stern patriot, which minimized all smaller weaknesses. Thus at last I entered into him.

He also expressed a 'vision' of doom:

After he has looked upon dead Caesar ..., the shadow of his
fate comes darkly upon Brutus. He is forcing himself to glory
in the deed, but the ghost of Caesar is before his eyes thenceforth
and ever saying, 'In vain! In vain!' ... His reason counters
feebly on his fate. He cries out against suicide as base and
cowardly, and then, with another fear at heart, asks one or
another to kill him, and then slays himself. All is lost. Portia is
dead, and only the immortal gods remain.

William Winter saw in Mansfield's performance a 'Brutus
almost spectral in spiritual conflict, fanatical self-absorption,
and silent, patient, majestic misery; ... the awful loneliness
of a great soul fated to disaster'.

The late Victorian is still the dominating manner of acting Shakespeare, with less time for preparation, and brought
up-to-date in detail. *The Times* has reported Dame Edith
Evans as telling a lecture audience that when she came to
study Volumnia she asked 'How could I possibly be a blood-
thirsty old harridan?'. She had 'found the woman', however, in Volumnia's love for Coriolanus; 'she adored Coriolanus':

When she meets her son after his triumph she is almost too
excited to be coherent. 'What is it? – Coriolanus must I call
thee?' In other words: 'What's this thing they have pinned on
you, darling? The V.C.?'

Shakespeare's plays have fostered this approach: 'How can
I be Hamlet? Touchstone? Viola? Lear? ...' In the performances of our finest actors and actresses, one after
another, lines spring into life, often contemporary life. Or a
face becomes defined. Sir Laurence Olivier has described
his search for Malvolio (Plate 21), a quest aware of Tree's
image and determined to find something new; the *Stratford-upon-Avon Herald* reported him as saying that

the part of Malvolio was dead, and something had to be done to it. He would walk round, looking at his barber or the man buying fish, searching for the way 'to break the traditional vase. For it has to be human; people have to understand'.

So this Malvolio appeared to the critic of *The Times* as a 'plain unlikeable man'; he was a vulgarian; he was reasonably annoyed; he both envied and despised his 'betters'. And Shakespeare's text carried this performance, Malvolio's last words sounding like the natural speech of a man who refuses to see himself as others see him, even if they are right.

There are perhaps three considerable additions to a Victorian actor's way of approaching a role. First is the virtuoso's, encouraged by Granville-Barker and by a scholarly esteem for Shakespeare's poetic artifice. Its apotheosis seems to have been nearly thirty years ago, in Sir John Gielgud's Richard II: the *Manchester Guardian* reported:

Mr Gielgud's face, growing more and more haggard with his eager woe, his voice ranging from a moving whisper to the highest pitch of his unavailing imperiousness, and most of all his hands, modelling the lines as they were delivered, and in themselves poetical, suave, and regal – these attributes made the character a shining monument to sorrow.

The other two new offerings to Shakespeare are more fashionable today. One is a rather innocent willingness to be directed by a 'director' who is held responsible for the 'meaning' or 'mood' of the whole play. This can demonstrate a light vitality or an eye-catching showmanship which is implicit in Shakespeare's writing; but quite rightly the chief object of the drama critics' praise or blame is often the director. The other is a new kind of patience, a responsible, slow, empirical, subtle search for a way of speaking and moving which is not circumscribed by a determination to define a dominant portrait, however original or complex. A few actors, influenced both by followers of Stanislavski and by a new scepticism, are prepared to work without precise aims and to let their audience remain puzzled. Charles Marowitz has reported in the *Observer* on Mr Paul Scofield's method of rehearsal for *King Lear* (Plate 22a):

Scofield's Lear has slowly begun to emerge. His method is to start from the text and work backwards. He is constantly testing the verse to see if the sound corresponds with the emotional intention. It is a peculiar method that consciously prods technique so that instinct will be called into play ... He frequently stammers his lines, openly testing inflexions and accents. ... What one sees is a man winding himself painfully into a Shakespearean fiction.

Sometimes it seems that the fortunes of the actors with Shakespeare are only just beginning. His plays have absorbed their attention and manifested their gifts in many ways – and to this abbreviated account of the English theatre should be added the long tally of performances in many other languages, for many different societies. But to the adventurous actor of talent, Shakespeare's plays always seem to withhold further, generous secrets.

SHAKESPEARE IN THE
MODERN THEATRE

Laurence Kitchin

PART from starry-eyed enthusiasts and theatre people with a vested interest, does anyone claim ever to have seen a fully satisfactory staging of Shakespeare? You would have needed to come away with the feeling you have after Glyndebourne Mozart, Moscow Chekhov, or East Berlin Brecht, that nothing much came between you and the author, that the stage was a mirror for his intentions. Not a perfect mirror, of course. The living audience would have coughed and breathed on it, but that would have been allowed for. The brilliance would have gained from it like breathed-on, polished glasses. A false note or a hesitation on stage would do no worse than point up the strength of the flow of impressions thrown back. After all, we don't have to pretend the stage is real, and not a mirror. But the modern stage's reflection of Shakespeare is always grossly tarnished. Rusty blotches still appear where survivors of the Edwardian ham tradition intone like toastmasters; or else a Theatre Workshop urbanite or a Method addict is suddenly landed with a speech the scholars have been dissecting for three hundred years; and then you see an ugly crack. When the man in charge, the director, is not sure what he wants

done with the verse and has not had practice in moving large numbers of actors about, the mirror disintegrates, leaving Shakespeare in fragments.

1945, the first year of the nuclear age, can be taken as a starting date for the modern English theatre. Towards the end of the second war a legendary standard of classical revivals was being set at the New and the Haymarket Theatres (Plate 22b). Both the companies concerned broke up, but not before Olivier's way of acting Shakespeare had lodged in the minds of young people as the one that got through to them better than anyone else's. It was, in the final analysis, no better than Gielgud's bland nineteen-thirtyish manner, but it was the one that caught on. Not only was Olivier's style widely circulated in films, but it survived the date many would choose as the start of the modern drama in England, that is 1956, the first year of the new playwrights. Olivier himself starred in one important new-wave play, John Osborne's *The Entertainer*, and married the star of another (Joan Plowright, who played Beatie in Arnold Wesker's *Roots*). During all these years, from 1956 until his appointment as Director of the National Theatre in 1963, Olivier played only two seasons at Stratford-upon-Avon and none at the other showcase for Shakespeare, the Old Vic. Of his brief West End seasons, one was at the now demolished St James's, where the view from the gallery was like peering down an elevator shaft, and the other at the vanished Stoll, of more than twice the size now thought suitable for acting and hearing a play. If we consider the movements of the most popular, and perhaps the greatest, of a great pre-war group of Shakespearian actors, two facts emerge. One is that no permanent company on the continental pattern collected round him; the other, that only a fraction of the public had a chance to see him in person. If this could happen to Olivier, it is no surprise to find a scarcity of Shakespeare performances among great actors and actresses of lesser personal magnetism. They found employment elsewhere, ageing steadily through films, television adaptations, recitals, and, most frustrating of all, sound broadcasts of roles they were no longer young enough to play in the theatre. The chief sufferers from this deprivation were the young: actors who might have learned from them on stage, and a public cheated of the easiest of all introductions to the Bard, the one given by star actors in person.

Beyond the simple, introductory aspect of live acting, one needs to remember that Shakespeare throws the main weight of his argument on the actor often enough, and he is assuming a man addressing a crowd. Films and television, which did not exist when the plays were written, are therefore agents of diffusion, substitutes like reproductions of a painting. But what about live performances in a foreign language? Many of us would rather have seen Vittorio Gassmann's Hamlet than Ian Bannen's without understanding a word of the translation, because the Italian's physique is ideal, and he has a historical sense, arrived at from long experience of acting his own country's classics. Instead, the British public was introduced to him as the sadistic thug (voice dubbed) in the film *Bitter Rice*. This incident, the living actor withheld and his filmed image widely diffused in a minor performance, is a valid symbol of drama in the 1950s, at any rate of its everyday background in a country too philistine to subsidize the best actors of its own best writer. Looking back, as many people in all walks of life are now doing, on the bomb-haunted, 'affluent' days of the fifties when Germany was building new theatres and England impotently mourning the loss of old ones, it now seems clear enough that a breakdown of insularity was exposing the set-up to widespread scrutiny for the first time. It began to be admitted that the neglect of a cultural, and for that matter commercial, asset of Shakespeare's stature was unusual in the modern world and uniquely British, like the rebuilding of the Memorial Theatre itself, half of it paid for by charitable Americans. Arguments in favour of the traditional inter-war teetering between haphazard West End revivals and an Old Vic run on the cheap began to sound like resistance to decimal coinage and a right-hand rule of the road. True, the conditions had produced a record harvest of Shakespeare actors, but they had ended in a sad waste of perishable talent. I have described the process elsewhere (*Essays and Studies of the English Association*, 1964; *Mid-Century Drama*, 1st edition, 1960. 2nd edition, 1962). The only cure for it, applied too recently for the results to be noticeable yet, was the elimination of the middleman, the commercial speculator, and the financing of live drama by national and municipal subsidy. Better late than never.

In this short survey of Shakespeare in the modern theatre, the scarcity of star acting when many star actors existed is the first thing to be borne in mind, if we think the plays have been disappointingly staged. There have been many fine performances, but too few in relation to the talent available. Not enough people have had the chance to see the best things of their kind, such as Olivier's Macbeth, Edith Evans's Nurse, Wolfit's Iago, Gielgud's Angelo, and Redgrave's Hamlet. The result is that audiences may be bored by these parts or, worse perhaps, be satisfied by weak performances of them. Either way it is unfair to the author and ultimately to the public. This top layer of glamour is only one aspect of the plays. Strip it off, however, and there may be a stampede to opera and ballet. It has, in fact, already occurred, as can be seen from the ticket queues for Callas, Fonteyn, or the Bolshoi. The trend is insidious. If anyone asked me to recommend a good mid-century Falstaff, I'd have to refer him to Geraint Evans in Verdi's opera.

When you get a shortage of Falstaffs, Antonys, Cleopatras, and Macbeths at roughly the same time in the playwright's native country, something happens to the image of the plays concerned, for all of them are roles essential to the structure. The mirror reflecting Shakespeare is blurred. Then some vigorous young actor is given one of the roles; and in the normal course of history he would have a giant model to copy, refine on, or reject; instead of which he will now have to make what he can of the text in the light of current acting theory. The theory may stress inner feeling (Strasberg) or significant action (Meisner), neither of which may reflect Shakespeare's handling of the part. Indeed the theory may stem from Moscow in Chekhov's time or New York of the New Deal epoch, perhaps both, whereas the air breathed by the Shakespeare character may be that of Tudor politics mixed with a literary notion of Roman gravity. Now and then the young actor's ignorance of tradition can be an advantage. Peter O'Toole, for example, had never seen any-one else in the part at the time of his excellent Shylock (Stratford, 1960; Plate 24a) and was able to draw on experience of the Jewish community in Leeds. More often, the gap between Shakespeare's world and the actor's environment yawns limply on stage. All that is left for him to do is remember any small-part hams he may happen to have seen and do the opposite. This is one form of incompetence protesting against another. With no giant model to cut his teeth on, he is like a disorientated adolescent without a father.

So far I have tried to indicate a link between discontinuity of experience and disappointing productions of Shakespeare. There was no equivalent of a bank in which accumulated know-how could be stored, the way Chekhov prompt copies are stored at the Moscow Art Theatre. At this point it may be as well to underline that the results really were dull and that the discontinuity existed. In 1959, John Fernald stated (*The Times*, 9 March): 'In general our drama is a messy sort of amorphous thing which is run on a shopkeeping basis, yet the people who are selling the goods are artists who could do wonderful things in a wonderful theatre.' Coming from the principal of the Royal Academy of Dramatic Art, this can be taken as an authoritative estimate of the gulf between potential and results. He went on to forecast that either we would have no theatre at all, or it would be run on a different basis. Just over a year later Peter Holmes, a young graduate actor who had just achieved a more than promising Tamburlaine for the Oxford University Dramatic Society, offered some data on discontinuity (*The Times*, 11 July 1960). He revealed that he had never seen Olivier, Gielgud, O'Toole, or Finney in person. Since the R.A.D.A. and the O.U.D.S. have always exerted a strong influence on Shakespeare acting, one would expect any dissatisfaction or confusion in those centres to be magnified elsewhere, for instance in the showcases at Stratford-upon-Avon and the Waterloo Road. It was.

Briefly, the Memorial Theatre was put on the map by Anthony Quayle, consolidated under Glen Byam Shaw, granted its Royal Charter and reformed to continental standards of efficiency under Peter Hall, by which time some of its best work was being done in London in fields other than Shakespeare. After its return from the West End to Waterloo Road, the Old Vic was no longer either an art theatre or a people's theatre and perished in the summer of 1963, nominally absorbed in the National Theatre. Some years before that, it became apparent that governmental dilatoriness in releasing the money promised for the National Theatre had forced the Old Vic and the Royal Shakespeare into cut-throat competition for the title. Although neither won it, nobody forced to comment on Shakespeare revivals during the contest will readily forget the disasters flowing from financial anxiety and over-stretched artistic resources. To these circumstances, further confused by the breach between two generations of actors, one may add the disruptive effects of the new drama of 1956 and the changes in habit caused by air travel and the mass media. From the point of view of the directors it must have seemed a near-miracle to mount Shakespeare at all, with so many actors caught up in a mosaic of engagements in two continents and four different performing media. However, there were signs of hunger to see Shakespeare acted all over the world, and the working rhythm of those who undertook to satisfy it resembled that of a flying sales-executive. The business world of Mr E. M. Forster's 'telegrams and anger' had evolved into ulcers and airports. Hall of the Royal Shakespeare developed a genius for personal publicity helpful to his organization; Benthall of the Old Vic became preoccupied with the problems of replacing half his company annually and of adjusting its pitch to the varying size of theatres in the U.S.A. Both companies began selling their productions to television, without, one hoped, being influenced by the possibility in their interpretation. All these things had become necessary, and all of them were subsidiary to the basic job of directing the plays with the attention they demanded. Talking to them for an hour or two, it was difficult to believe that Hall had once directed *Waiting for Godot* and Benthall *The White Devil*, with great artistic success. In the struggle to market Shakespeare in the affluent society they had acquired an impersonal, executive gloss. And sometimes a hard streamlining crept into the plays, notably in *Twelfth Night*, which withers under insensitive handling and has unjustly become one of the biggest bores in the repertory, along with *A Midsummer Night's Dream*. The recurrent fault of revivals at both showcase theatres was the lack of a sense of conviction on stage, of the energy throbbing in every corner of a Russian or Brechtian ensemble. Finding most of the middle-part actors at Stratford and the Old Vic unaccountably stodgy, I decided it could be the result of regimentation and fatigue. Something in their faces seemed to assert that they were word-perfect, on time, in the right place, and what more could you expect, the way we live now?

Matters like theatre policy and the availability of actors ought not to enter the mind of anyone out to enjoy Shakespeare in the theatre. Like health, they only become a talking point when something is wrong. In the modern English theatre, packed with promising dramatists and an exceptional crop of young actors, some of the menace to good Shakespeare has come from changes in society not necessarily philistine in intent. More of it has come from an effete idea of the drama as genteel after-dinner amusement, a meeting place of snobbish social insiders and their deferential entertainers. One day it will be recognized as grotesque that for so many years the London headquarters of our great dramatist was poorly based on what was then very much the unfashionable side of the river, and financed on a shoestring, picturesquely close to the Cut, the costermongers, and so on. For all the Old Vic's achievements and value as a springboard to the West End and Hollywood, few of the alumni were in any great hurry to go back. Given less sentimental lip-service and more money between the wars, the Old Vic might have conserved the tradition of Shakespeare in the way Paris looked after Molière. The stiffest of Comédie Française revivals never drops beyond a minimum authority in understanding and technique. At least the high-pressure methods of Hall and Benthall lifted Shakespeare production out of its insular groove and gave it social status, too much in terms of Dallas and Birmingham subtopia, no doubt, but of its time, and free from the air of eccentric charity which hung over the pre-war Old Vic and some of the most illustrious provincial reps. Hall went further; he introduced what had long been the opportunist manager's nightmare – though normal practice abroad – the long-term contract.

There could have been only one alternative preferable to a ruthless streamlining of the Shakespeare industry in the

1950s, and it would have been utopian. It would have required a fanatical genius, able to seduce a large company of exceptional actors from screen assignments long enough to weld them into an ensemble. Then, with a suitable building available, the plays could have been given the careful, searching preparation they deserve. There would have been Glyndebourne standards for Shakespeare, as there certainly were for Chekhov at the first Chichester festival of 1962. It might have been in the interests of Shakespeare if Hall had been content to mark time at Stratford long enough to evolve a truly expert ensemble, instead of extending the company's activities to London and its repertory to Brecht and the European avant-garde. Equally to him and to Benthall, a major source of frustration and expense was the buildings they had inherited. The stages of both invited spectacular pictorial effects; and it was assumed, rightly or wrongly, that any renunciation of these facilities would be punished at the box office. The assumption was wrong, if we are to judge from the ascetic screens designed by Peter Brook for the successful *King Lear* of 1962, but it led to anxious undertakings like Zeffirelli's sumptuous Venetian designs for *Othello*, obstructive on the first night at Stratford and too big for transfer to the Aldwych. About the design of the present Royal Shakespeare Theatre (Plate 26b) for suitable staging of Shakespeare, the less said the better. It was opened in 1932, and its flashy provincialism jars against the elegance and utility of Glyndebourne, which began to evolve only two years later. The contrast expresses an insular attitude to Shakespeare, alongside grand opera's contact with Europe.

In spite of erratic artistic standards, the Hall régime has played a big part in closing that gap, not only by removing classical actors from the hazards of casual labour but by the installation of Michel Saint-Denis and Peter Brook, two of the world's best directors, as his partners. Through all the intrigues and pressures tied up with the 'prestige' drama in the nuclear age, the likely evolution here would be towards a triumvirate, with Hall the administrator, Brook the director of plays, and Saint-Denis the trainer of actors. Given reasonable freedom from stress it would ensure high standards automatically, but nothing in the record of those concerned leads one to hope for exclusive concentration on Shakespeare. Looking at it from Shakespeare's point of view, as perhaps one should in this fourth-centenary year, he has no home, certainly not the National Theatre with its new-wave directorate. In a way, the universal genius who belongs to everyone, belongs to nobody. After some expensive, well-meaning travesty, the critic is sometimes called on to share an eager tourist's enthusiasm for what has been done, and then the impulse is to tell them that the faint whirring up-river is not hydro-electric, but the Bard revolving in his grave.

In the great showcases of what one might call expense-account Shakespeare, the pace is hectic and a state of emergency frequent. For example, the Royal Shakespeare's *King Lear* of 1962 had to be postponed for a month on the orders of Paul Scofield's doctor. The stop-gap turned out to be the most literate and stylish *Comedy of Errors* in living memory, one of the company's biggest artistic successes. The reputations of Alec McCowen and his director, Clifford Williams, rose several points. Yet one hopes for a middle way between the Moscow Art Theatre's five-year stint on *The Winter's Tale* and this inspired conjuring trick. Somehow the showcases will have to provide conditions in which the more exacting masterpieces can be worked on in calm deliberation, so as not to miss the glacial silences at the core, Shakespeare's equivalent of a late Beethoven quartet. They occur often in the tragedies, but also in *Twelfth Night*, though you would scarcely suspect it from recent productions. The lack of this quality is one of the factors that makes Olivier's Hamlet so much inferior to Forbes-Robertson's as seen in the 1913 film. As he is the bridge between two generations of actors, Olivier's excellence in busy, extrovert roles has joined with the city-street rhythm of the new dramatists and made it very difficult for anyone to express withdrawn moods in Shakespeare. The mid-century Hamlet says, 'Now I am alone', in the only way he knows – like an executive with two spare minutes to swallow his Equanil between appointments. Shakespeare's meant it like Raleigh in the Tower.

One other aspect of prestige Shakespeare should be mentioned and that is the Stratford, Ontario, experiment (Plates 27a and b). This was the fanatical idea of Tom Patterson – according to Tyrone Guthrie (*A Life in the Theatre*, 1960) 'a small mouse-coloured person' – but with shrewdness enough to call in the greatest director of Shakespeare since Granville-Barker. Like the American share of the building costs of the Memorial Theatre, Patterson's initiative exposes the philistine indifference to Shakespeare of the Establishment English, supposedly his cultural trustees. What Guthrie wanted, had already obtained in Scotland (Edinburgh Festival, 1948), and now had in Canada, was an approximation to Shakespeare's own public stage, modified in the light of modern requirements; no antiquarian reconstruction but an efficient machine for acting, hearing, and seeing the plays. That was in 1953, half a century after the need for something of the kind had been a cliché of artistic opinion, beginning with William Poel. Not until 1962 was the first modern open-stage theatre built in England for the Chichester Festival. By that time Guthrie was heavily committed in Minnesota. So the English never provided the best living director of Shakespeare with the requisite tools for his job. Instead, they gave him a knighthood. And all this time the office blocks had been climbing steadily.

If this survey has a random, haphazard air, the subject

insists on it, because Shakespeare is staged today in an atmosphere of crisis. Even the optics of live theatre are changing, under the influence of television and the cinema. Things taken for granted only ten years ago – galleries, crush bars, anonymous criticism – are suddenly questioned, and revealed as archaic. One thing seems clear. The unpopular idea that Shakespeare reads better than he plays has weight behind it, in so far as it grows from attending bad productions. Drama in the U.S.A. has not taken a course which is much help to Shakespeare acting; the Method suits another kind of play. In England, on the other hand, the experience and the talent have still to be concentrated. Shakespeare's plays demand large casts, at home with Tudor diction and behaviour. When Ben Jonson wrote, 'He was not of an age, but for all time', he gave lazy directors a licence to cut down the plays to their own size. Shakespeare is for all time, but also an Elizabethan who needs understanding as such. Perhaps the greatest handicap to the modern English theatre has been the expensiveness and scarcity of Granville-Barker's *Prefaces to Shakespeare*, remedied in 1963 by editions in paperback, with authoritative notes and illustrations by Muriel St Clare Byrne. These remain the best guide for directors. If they had been more widely available, we would have been spared a thousand solecisms.

To release their full power in the theatre, these plays need a dedicated group which holds together under inspired leadership. The nearest I felt to Shakespeare in the last ten years was not in a first-night stall, but on a canvas chair in a Pimlico youth club, watching what is now the National Youth Theatre rehearsing for the Paris Festival (Plate 23b). True ensemble depends on the actors knowing one another and their director's approach so well that nothing has to be spelt out. At one point in this rehearsal the Hamlet was missing, away for a brief costume check. Michael Croft called a name, and a swarthy teenager from Burnley at once took the floor and went through the scene, word-perfect. This company had absolute confidence in the text. They behaved as if it would shelter their youth and inexperience as effectively in the Théâtre Sarah-Bernhardt as it had already done in the West End; and they were right. 'If you can't beat them, join them' is a better attitude than most to the rhythms of Shakespearian verse.

SHAKESPEARE IN
FILM, RADIO, AND
TELEVISION

John Russell Taylor

HATEVER else he may or may not have been, Shakespeare was certainly one of the world's great story-tellers, and his qualities as such have been appreciated at times and in places when these were the only qualities of his which could be appreciated. Like Homer, Virgil, Boccaccio, and Chaucer he found his material here, there, and everywhere, but left his mark indelibly upon it, and, as with them, his works were both an end and a beginning; an end in themselves as finished works of art, and a beginning as an inexhaustible quarry of plot-material for other artists with other ends in view.

Thus it was natural that as each new artistic medium emerged Shakespeare should be laid under tribute if it was at all conceivable, and certainly if there was plot material to be found. In the seventeenth century the English opera-masque produced in Purcell's *The Fairy Queen* (vaguely based on *A Midsummer Night's Dream*) and *The Tempest* its two most lasting contributions to the musical stage. In the eighteenth century, with the rise of literary criticism as we understand the term today (what Mr George Watson calls 'descriptive criticism') as a respectable literary form

Shakespeare was rivalled only by Homer as a subject for dissertation. In the nineteenth century it was the turn of grand opera, and in *Otello* and *Falstaff* Verdi brought to Shakespearian themes a genius almost matching Shakespeare's own; if one could hardly say the same of most proponents of the programme symphony and the symphonic poem (despite Berlioz's *Romeo and Juliet*), the ripe romanticism of Tchaikovsky's *Hamlet* and *Romeo and Juliet* has probably not even now exhausted its subliminal influence, and certainly lingers on to colour practically every balletic interpretation of Shakespeare, whether Western and psychological, like Robert Helpmann's *Hamlet* (set, incidentally, to the Tchaikovsky music) or eastern and anecdotal, like the Prokoviev-Lavrovsky *Romeo and Juliet*.

With this long and often distinguished history of Shakespeare transposed, it was only to be expected that the characteristically twentieth-century media would also have a go at Shakespeare. Not only does he offer raw material with a useful array of built-in associations which the adapter and embroiderer may hope to gather as a little bonus of unearned artistic income, but – which is obviously useful where a new medium is trying to establish itself as culturally respectable – he also carries an invaluable cultural cachet: there is a feeling abroad that when the film, radio, television, and gramophone record are ready to tackle Shakespeare, they are ready also to be taken seriously by serious people. Prizes for special endeavour from inside and outside the art-industries concerned tend to be heaped on their efforts to grapple with Shakespeare: it was a foregone conclusion that the B.B.C.'s series of Shakespeare histories *An Age of Kings* would carry off most of the year's television prizes, quite apart from its merits, and it can hardly be coincidental that one of the few major Oscars of the Hollywood Motion Picture Academy to be won by an all-British film went to Laurence Olivier for his *Hamlet*. Even if the public does not support such ventures as enthusiastically as it might (which occasionally happens) they can always be written off as prestige-getters and the blame laid for once fairly and squarely (or at least squarely, if not always fairly) at the public's door.

Before we start to consider the chequered career of Shakespeare in these new media, however, there is one thing worth pointing out. Though like all theatre Shakespeare's drama is a visual art, and even has its occasional purely visual *coups de théâtre* (the descent of the 'statue' of Hermione from her pedestal near the end of *The Winter's Tale*, for instance), the prime accent is on sound rather than sight; scenes are set by what we hear, not what we see, and many of the most familiar passages of Shakespeare are long speeches, like Hamlet's soliloquies, Jacques's Seven Ages of Man speech, Ulysses's discourse on Order, Enobarbus's 'The barge she sat in ...', which present virtually nothing for the physical eye to see at all. These are not all Shakespeare, or anything like it, but on the other hand they are essential to Shakespeare; you can't just take them away on the grounds that if Shakespeare had been writing for the modern theatre, with all its resources, or for the cinema, he would not have written like that. Or at least you can, but in doing so you run into the obvious difficulty that your audiences may refuse to recognize the result as 'Shakespeare' any more, and if this happens you have thrown away all the built-in advantages, to replace them probably only with resentment and suspicion.

Now it stands to reason that the more the medium you are dealing with inclines to expression in primarily visual terms, the more you are going to be dogged by this difficulty. Especially if it is a new medium, not yet quite established in respectable opinion as an art in its own right. If you put on an opera called *Othello* or a ballet called *Hamlet* nobody is going to complain very loudly that 'It isn't Shakespeare';

of course it isn't – it's opera or ballet first, and the fact that the theme comes from Shakespeare is more or less coincidental. At worst audiences may complain, as with Andrée Howard's ballet *Twelfth Night* a few years back, that the plot is too involved to be conveyed satisfactorily in terms of ballet, or something of the sort. But offer a film or a radio production called *Othello* or *Hamlet* which omits or rewrites a lot of Shakespeare's text and you will probably be in for trouble; on the credits of the first talking Shakespeare film, *The Taming of the Shrew*, with Mary Pickford and Douglas Fairbanks, the fateful note, 'additional dialogue by Sam Taylor', caused such a flurry that it has not yet been forgotten.

This means that the new media best calculated to swallow Shakespeare whole without indigestion are the purely aural ones, radio and the gramophone record. Film, though not – as the older pundits, brought up in the silent cinema, would have us believe – almost exclusively a visual art, is still visual to an extent which makes wholesale transfer of Shakespeare from stage to screen a dangerous undertaking. Television, still the newest and least formed of the four, hovers awkwardly in between, enjoying some of the advantages of radio and suffering from some of the film's disadvantages where Shakespeare is concerned. It is not surprising, therefore, that radio and the gramophone seem up to now to have acclimatized Shakespeare most successfully. There are at least two complete recordings of Shakespeare's works on long-playing records under way in this country, both offering uncut texts and a minimum of discreet background music and effects. This unobtrusive 'adaptation', almost always with some cutting to fit in with programme schedules, has generally been found the most effective way of putting Shakespeare on radio, and in the course of its existence B.B.C. radio has presented on one or other of its three domestic channels productions along these lines of all Shakespeare's plays but two, *Titus Andronicus* and (rather surprisingly) *The Comedy of Errors* – though this latter, with all its juggling with two pairs of identical twins, might reasonably claim to be the most visual of all Shakespeare's plays. The most popular of Shakespeare's plays on radio to date has been *The Tempest*, with no fewer than fourteen full-scale productions; after that came *Twelfth Night* with eleven, *Hamlet* with nine, and *Othello*, *The Merchant of Venice*, and *Romeo and Juliet* with seven each.

Television, though in its pre-war beginnings almost as educationally orientated as sound radio, has tended until recently to fight shy of Shakespeare in Britain, and even more so in America, apart from one or two wild prestige productions in early days, when everything was done live and all sorts of things could go terribly wrong (Maurice Evans has some scarifying stories of his renowned television *Hamlet* in New York). The first full-scale Shakespeare production on television seems to have been the B.B.C.'s modern-dress *Julius Caesar* in July 1938; a few months later they relayed a stage production of *Twelfth Night* complete from the Phoenix Theatre and then shortly before the wartime shutdown they did a full-dress studio production of *The Tempest*. After the war things began again slowly, and television Shakespeare, despite isolated attempts on both B.B.C. and Independent channels, cannot be said really to have caught on until the B.B.C.'s ambitious series of Shakespeare histories in 1960 under the general title *An Age of Kings*. This took up an idea previously tried on sound radio: that of treating the main body of Shakespeare's history-plays from *Richard II* to *Richard III* as a coherent sequence with a continuity of theme running right through. The texts were somewhat cut (particularly in the *Henry VI* plays) and rearranged into fifteen episodes running in regular series from April to November, with the same actors playing the same parts throughout and the same producer and director (Michael Hayes and Peter Dews respectively) in charge of the whole series. A similar arrangement was essayed in 1963 with the classical history plays, grouped under the title *The Spread of the Eagle*.

An Age of Kings probably offers the fairest ground to date for judging television's potential in adapting Shakespeare; certainly it is the most extensive. Television, it is often said, is an intimate medium for watching in intimate, familial surroundings. This is to a large extent true (as it is, incidentally, of radio). Television is also a visual medium, and this means that if it does not have necessarily to convey its meaning largely or entirely in visual terms, it does at least have to keep the eyes occupied, because if the eyes wander the mind wanders too. Both of these qualities are in themselves mixed blessings where Shakespeare is concerned, and moreover each complicates the problems which arise from the other. The first means that quiet, intimate scenes are in general better suited to television than expansive rhetorical scenes, Richard II's more introspective moments rather than Henry V's clarion calls to arms. Effects can of course be graded, as they can on radio, by varying the distance of the speaker from microphone and camera, but here the visual nature of the medium steps in to complicate matters. If you hold an actor in close-up while he soliloquizes you are likely – unless the actor commands a quite exceptional degree of personal magnetism – to find your audience's attention drifting because one face in close-up for some length of time is not all that interesting to watch. Equally, if you move your actor far enough away for the big, demonstrative moments he is likely on the normal home screen to be so small and insignificant-looking that again he cannot magnetize attention. And if you do everything in medium shot it will just look dull anyway. (This last was the pitfall *An Age of Kings* most often fell into.)

But put like that, this argument seems to suggest that all drama should be impossible on television. This obviously is not true, but what it really resolves itself into is more than anything a matter of timing. Television must be able to mix up close, medium, and long shots, to move cameras around a lot or have a lot happening in front of them. Most stage-plays offer possibilities of all of these things, but as it were in slow motion; they dwell in moods that television should ideally just touch on, they take time to make transitions which television can do in a flash. There is hardly a stage play written of which the author, once properly schooled in television techniques, could not equally well convey the essence for television in an hour.

Does this then mean that Shakespeare and other classics should not be done on television at all? Strictly speaking, yes, that is precisely what it does mean – that no plays should be performed on television but those written for television; swift, fluid, *nuancé*. But clearly no one is going to speak as strictly as that. Even if the effect of Shakespeare on the television screen is, even at its very best, considerably less than in a passable stage performance, television production still has a number of advantages other than strictly aesthetic: for instance, the number of people who can see a single performance (it is estimated that more people saw the Royal Shakespeare Company's television *As You Like It* in March 1963 during one showing than had previously seen the play during its whole earlier history on the stage), and the durability of a taped production as a record. Shakespeare on television still has a lot to offer, provided we know clearly in advance just what we may hope to get out of it.

In other words, we have to accept that with television it is not a simple choice of whether everything which happens on the small screen is art or nothing that happens there is (it is certainly arguable that television cannot in any case be an art on its own, but merely a particular form of various other arts); sometimes it may be, sometimes not, and a television production of a Shakespeare play, even if it cannot be television with a capital *t*, is not necessarily for that reason altogether without value. This sort of consideration is involved in an even more acute form, though, when we come to the film and its relations with Shakespeare, for the film has excellent claims to be considered an art in its own right: as good, certainly, as those of ballet or opera. And if we can feel sure in our own minds that the film is an art form (sure in a way that we cannot be with television) then our distress, or at least confusion of mind, when we feel that it is not fulfilling its artistic potential is likely to be all the greater. And this is precisely what is likely to happen when Shakespeare is brought to the screen.

Now there are two schools of thought about how screen Shakespeare should be tackled. They are often assumed to be mutually exclusive, but are not really; on the other hand it is important that the film-maker should decide clearly which he is following in any specific instance. Basically they can be reduced to two propositions: (1) that it is the film-maker's job to record Shakespeare; and (2) that it is the film-maker's job, if he is going to tackle Shakespeare at all, to put the requirements of the film medium first and pay as little attention to the letter as a composer or choreographer would. The two views are not, as they seem, mutually exclusive; they merely reflect two perfectly proper functions that the cinema can perform.

Consider for a moment a different field of activity: dancing and the film. Obviously on the one hand the film offers the choreographer all sorts of possibilities which the stage does not allow him; it postulates a form of ballet which may be based on the concerted movements of a group of dancers or the movements of one dancer's whole body, as on a stage, but may also make use of emphases the stage cannot manage on a single arm or leg, a facial expression, or may actively involve the spectator (as represented by the camera-eye) in the dance. But the film can also be an invaluable unvarnished record, and is used as such by a number of companies these days: a simple record shot from one position, usually the centre of the dress circle, of the complete ballet as performed in the theatre. Either use of the cinema is perfectly legitimate, but only the first has anything to do with cinema art; where the trouble and the complaints from both ballet and cinema purists come in is when no clear decision is taken about which the film-maker is aiming for, and some hybrid emerges which is satisfactory neither as film nor as record but partakes a little of both.

With this distinction in mind we may perhaps see the muddled progress of Shakespeare in the cinema more clearly. Obviously the same two possibilities exist for a satisfactory relationship between Shakespeare and the film medium as for ballet and film: on the one hand the record, on the other the transformation. And where most film-makers faced with Shakespeare have gone wrong is in their failure to decide clearly between the two. Clearly a simple record of a memorable production is possible; indeed often most desirable. We should not pretend to ourselves that it would be readily viewable as entertainment by the average audience, any more than the record-films in the Royal Ballet's files would be; a film record of, say, Gielgud's Hamlet, Peggy Ashcroft's Cleopatra, or Scofield's Lear, shot uncompromisingly from a single viewpoint, would be unbearably dull to almost anyone except the theatrical historian; but to him how valuable and to the rest of us, in small extracts at least, how fascinating it could be at some future date. In theory, indeed, the filming need not be quite so strict as this, since so much of the skill of stage direction lies in judging ways of doing what the film's changing camera set-ups do automatically: focusing attention on the right part of the stage picture at the right time; but the cost of varying the camera's point of view in what must necessarily be a non-commercial piece of filming would be prohibitive.

Anyway, talk of the cinema's potential as a purely recording medium is to date largely theoretical, despite the hopes and plans of the British Theatre Museum Association. On the rare occasions the cinema has been used simply to record, it has mainly been inadvertently and for want of the imagination to do anything else. It happened once or twice in early days: with Cecil Hepworth's film of *Hamlet* starring Forbes-Robertson in 1913 and based, as far as it went, fairly closely on Forbes-Robertson's current stage production; or with the three Shakespeare films Beerbohm Tree made, of parts of *King John* in 1899, *Henry VIII* in 1911, and *Macbeth* (with Constance Collier as Lady Macbeth) in 1916. In any case the value of these films as records, interesting though in small doses they are, is considerably diminished by their being silent, even though the gramophone can to some extent fill the gap and tell us as well what Forbes-Robertson and Tree sounded like.

But for the most part, even from the earliest times some attempt was made to turn Shakespeare into cinema. Already before 1910 a large number of Shakespeare films had been made (the combination of popularity and cultural cachet was clearly irresistible), among them versions of several plays never subsequently attempted, like *Measure for Measure*, *The Winter's Tale*, and *The Comedy of Errors* (though a Rodgers and Hart musical remotely derived from the last, *The Boys from Syracuse*, was filmed in 1940). The closeness of these films to the original plays may be gauged from the fact that as well as being silent they were almost without exception only one or two reels long (i.e. ten or twenty minutes). Most were of no particular distinction or even interest except to the film historian; but one might mention Clément Maurice's record of Bernhardt's Duel Scene from

Hamlet, made for the Paris Exhibition of 1900; Georges Méliès's two Shakespeare snippets of 1907, *Shakespeare Writing Julius Caesar* (with Caesar's death) and *Hamlet and the Jester's Skull*; a D. W. Griffith *Taming of the Shrew* in 1908 with Florence Lawrence playing Katharina; and Vitagraph's ambitious three-reel version of *As You Like It* in 1912, for which Rose Coughlin repeated (at the age of 62) her famous stage performance as Rosalind.

The rest of the silent period brought little either exciting or controversial; admittedly, since it was impossible to use Shakespeare's words anyway, there was little for people to argue about, save possibly the propriety of Asta Nielsen's interesting new interpretation of *Hamlet* in 1921, at the end of which the secret of the gloomy Dane turned out to be that he was a woman all the time (Plate 28a). Lubitsch's *Romeo and Juliet* in 1920 was felt to be a little heavy and plebeian (this was before he went to Hollywood and became the high-priest of sophisticated comedy); but Emil Jannings's *Othello*, directed by Dimitri Buchetowetski, captured at least something of what was obviously a remarkable performance. Otherwise there were no major attempts to transfer Shakespeare to the screen until the very end of the silent cinema, when *The Taming of the Shrew* (1929, Plate 28b) with Mary Pickford and Douglas Fairbanks was made in two versions, one silent, the other all-talking. Though many good judges then and since have thought the silent version better, it was the sound version which was most widely shown, and it was not a great success. Douglas Fairbanks was in principle happily cast as the roistering Petruchio, but more adept at the business than at delivering Shakespeare's lines; Mary Pickford, in one of her bolder attempts to get away from the golden-haired image of the world's sweetheart, was more intelligent than forceful as Katharina and fell back on the device (not unknown, it must be admitted, on the stage) of making it clear that Katharina knew from the start what Petruchio was up to and played along with him. Apart from this deviation, Sam Taylor's adaptation was quite straightforward and conventional.

When the film did not catch on with the public the idea of making talking pictures of Shakespeare was promptly shelved for some six years, apart from one or two star turns in revue-films (John Barrymore as Richard III in Warner Brothers' *Show of Shows*; Norma Shearer and John Gilbert in the Balcony Scene from *Romeo and Juliet* in M.G.M.'s *Hollywood Parade*, first playing it straight, then guying it). The main reason for this delay, though, would seem to be a sudden realization on the part of film-makers that Shakespeare films with dialogue introduced all sorts of new complications: the horror with which that 'additional dialogue by Sam Taylor' was received showed clearly enough that the adapter had to tread more warily here than anywhere else. And indeed when the next full-scale cinematic attack on Shakespeare appeared, Cukor's *Romeo and Juliet* with Norma Shearer and Leslie Howard as a rather mature pair of teenage lovers, great stress was placed in advertising it on the line 'Every word is Shakespeare's' (what little 'additional dialogue' was required being pieced together laboriously from other works). In the same year, 1935, there were two other attempts, Paul Czinner's *As You Like It*, made in England with Elizabeth Bergner and Laurence Olivier, and Max Reinhardt's extravagant Hollywood version of *A Midsummer Night's Dream*. And these three films at once show some of the dilemmas in which the screen adapter of Shakespeare must find himself.

Two of the three, *Romeo and Juliet* and *As You Like It*, took the line of least resistance: they filmed the text carefully and soberly, cut like most stage productions but obtrusively 'respected'. One can find fault with the casting, of course – the arguments against the Shearer–Howard combination are self-evident, though within their limitations they both do an able professional job; Elizabeth Bergner's German accent and winsome ways are a bit too much for most English audiences – but so one can with most stage productions. Cinematically too one can find fault, but the solutions adopted to each problem are always perfectly respectable: if the result of filming Shakespeare straight in solid chunks with only the barest pretence of rendering him 'cinematic' is a bit stodgy and dull, at least critics and audiences may be relied on to think that it is stodgy and dull in a good cause, culture being in any case, as everyone knows, more likely to be a penance than a pleasure. (It is worth noting, incidentally, that the best performance in either film, John Barrymore's Mercutio, is the most un-ashamedly stagey: the Queen Mab speech is delivered straight into the camera without any attempt at pretending that it is 'cinema'.)

The version of *A Midsummer Night's Dream* directed by Reinhardt with the assistance of William Dieterle (who was shortly afterwards, in *The Hunchback of Notre Dame*, to translate the Reinhardt spirit most successfully on to film) is a very different kettle of fish. Here the casting is not merely questionable, but downright fantastic, with James Cagney as Bottom, Mickey Rooney as Puck, and Dick Powell as Lysander. Moreover, though the film ran for 140 minutes, or as long as the average stage production, it managed to jettison more than half of the text and make room for most of Mendelssohn's incidental music accompanying lengthy ballet-sequences featuring numerous fairies clad in lamé seaweed (Plate 29b) and – an extraordinary invention this – an elongating cloak for Oberon under which, in the dawn sequence, all the fairies manage to cluster. Not, clearly, a 'serious' approach to Shakespeare at all, and yet, strange to relate, a remarkably successful film, one which even today is fresh and vivid when its more worthy, respectable con-temporaries look hopelessly faded. However dubious it may all look on paper, in the cinema it nearly all works. The performances, if sometimes a trifle odd, are lively and interesting, and Mickey Rooney's Puck is absolutely brilliant. The fairy sequences in particular, shot through spangled gauze for the most part, distil precisely the slightly cruel, slightly sinister poetry that Shakespeare achieved in words, often by cutting the words and replacing them with visual equivalents of startling beauty. Oddly enough, Reinhardt the stage director has in his only film managed to do what most experienced film directors have hardly considered doing: he has translated Shakespeare instead of merely recording him.

There is no point in trailing gloomily through all the other film adaptations of Shakespeare since 1935. We have had respectable versions from abroad (a French *The Merchant of Venice* with Michel Simon, a Russian *Twelfth Night*); film versions of ballets based on Shakespeare (Ulanova in *Romeo and Juliet*, a bizarre Georgian *Othello*); a marvellously elegant and sophisticated puppet-film of *A Midsummer Night's Dream* from Czechoslovakia; two brave 16-mm. adaptations from America; and a number of attempts at up-dated versions of Shakespeare stories – Kurosawa's Japanese *Macbeth*, *Throne of Blood*, and an Anglo-American gangster version, *Joe Macbeth*; Chabrol's *Ophelia* and Kaütner's *The Rest is Silence*, both based on *Hamlet*; and, most interesting and attractive, a science-fiction *The Tempest* called *The Lost Planet*, in which Ariel became a friendly robot and Caliban a creature from the exiled Professor's Id. There have also been, for the connoisseur, flashes of bizarre casting in films about actors: Bette Davis as Juliet in *It's Love I'm After*; Ophelias from Gertrude Lawrence in *Men Are Not Gods* to Margaret Lockwood in *The Man in Grey*; Ronald Colman's Othello in *A Double Life* and, as living proof that comedians should not succumb to their traditional urge to play Hamlet, Chaplin's rendering of 'To be, or not to be . . .' in *A King in New York*.

But for practical purposes the Shakespeare adaptations worth taking seriously reduce themselves to eight: three by Laurence Olivier, *Henry V*, *Hamlet*, and *Richard III*; two by Orson Welles, *Macbeth* and *Othello*; Joseph Mankiewicz's *Julius Caesar*; Renato Castellani's *Romeo and Juliet*, and Sergei Yutkevitch's *Othello*. The Castellani *Romeo and Juliet* can be quickly disposed of: it was originally meant to be an adaptation of the story on which Shakespeare based his play, and would no doubt have been better that way – the pictures were beautiful but the acting appalling. This apart, the films divide themselves into the 'faithful' – *Julius Caesar* and the Yutkevitch *Othello* – and the 'creative' – the two Welles films – with the Olivier films somewhere in between. Yutkevitch's *Othello* (Plate 29a), filmed in Russian, follows the text very closely and represents probably the best that can be done with presenting a faithful record palatably; the play, being one of Shakespeare's least reflective, offers no obvious difficulties in the way of set speeches or atmospheric writing which the cinema must inevitably render otiose, and the director records it in a series of compositions of extraordinary vividness and power, photographed in some of the most beautiful colour ever seen in the cinema. Mankiewicz's *Julius Caesar* (Plate 30a), despite some good and some odd casting (it has John Gielgud as Cassius and Marlon Brando magnetic but wrong as Antony, who is anything but the good-guy doing his best in a difficult situation here presented) seems to me, I must confess, a little insipid, respectable certainly but in the final analysis unexciting.

Altogether more interesting are the three Olivier films. Least so, I think, is *Richard III*, which is the nearest to the 'faithful' school and fails to establish any consistent style at all. *Henry V* (Plates 30b and 31a) on the other hand, establishes several styles which just do not fit together: the opening is shown as on the stage of the Globe, but later we accept the Chorus's invitation to escape its confines in our imagination and wander abroad in still evidently non-realistic surroundings (suggested largely by medieval illuminations), and then are suddenly launched on a completely realistic Battle of Agincourt. Each part is well enough done in its way, and some of it very well indeed (surely never except in the middle of the last war can Henry have been seen so readily in a completely heroic light), but the film fails as a whole because it never manages to synthesize its various elements. For this reason I personally prefer *Hamlet* (Plate 31b), though the central role is of the three the least suited to Olivier's particular gifts as an actor. At least the film does establish a consistent visual style – with its silky black-and-white, its constant use of deep-focus photography – and a powerful atmosphere. The soliloquies are still a problem, and not quite solved, though the efforts at making them partly interior monologue are a brave try at translating instead of merely recording.

For a real lesson in the art of translation, though, one has to turn to Orson Welles. Welles's *Macbeth* is a special case, made deliberately cheaply and quickly in order to exorcize some bee in his bonnet about a cinematic equivalent of the repertory theatre: it has its moments but really comes into its own only in the last reel, when Shakespeare is cheerfully thrown out of the window and instead we are given a good uninhibited film battle. On the other hand Welles's *Othello* seems to me triumphantly successful, and by far the best Shakespeare film ever made (Reinhardt's *A Midsummer Night's Dream* comes a good second). In it Welles puts the film first, and literal fidelity to Shakespeare's text virtually nowhere. He assumes, as the deviser of a Shakespeare ballet would naturally assume, that we know the plot already, and what he presents is therefore not a laborious exposition of the plot but a series of dazzling baroque variations on it. Someone who went into the cinema knowing nothing whatever of the play and its story would soon be completely lost in the film, which contains only snippets half-obscured by the camera's loving explorations of Venetian architecture, its extravagant movements in and out among the actors, picking up only a word here, a phrase there; indeed, to make matters worse the film starts with a long pre-credits sequence showing the funeral of Othello and Desdemona and the punishment of Iago before the innocent spectator has any idea who they are and what has happened.

But if one agrees that it is fair to assume some elementary plot-knowledge beforehand, then Welles's film comes into its own. It does not record, but offers instead a sort of cinematic equivalent to the Shakespearian experience, using all the resources of the modern cinema to do so. With Welles's *Othello* the cinema, for the first time really in its dealings with Shakespeare, summons up the confidence to regard itself as an art in its own right, using even Shakespeare as raw material to be chopped and changed and adapted entirely according to the cinema's artistic requirements. A shocking idea? Perhaps; what might happen in the hands of a lesser talent than Orson Welles one hesitates to think. But with him one can happily say, as one could say of Verdi's *Otello* too, that if Shakespeare would not recognize and approve of the result, then the less Shakespeare he.

SHAKESPEARE
IN CELEBRATION

Stanley Wells and
T. J. B. Spencer

'THE birthdays of such men as Shakespeare', wrote Leigh Hunt, 'ought to be kept, in common gratitude and affection, like those of relations whom we love.' The sentiment is shared by many; but there have been dissentient voices – George Bernard Shaw's for instance: 'I have long ago ceased to celebrate my own birthday; and I do not see why I should celebrate Shakespeare's. Whoever expects me to put myself, every 23 April, in an attitude at all differing from my attitude on 23 October, is doomed to disappointment.' But even Shaw, some years later, softened so far as to travel to Stratford-upon-Avon for the birthday celebrations and to propose the toast to the Immortal Memory at the official luncheon. Thus the man who had once written of Shakespeare 'the intensity of my impatience with him occasionally reaches such a pitch, that it would positively be a relief to me to dig him up and throw stones at him', linked himself with the many people who for a long time have felt impelled periodically to put themselves in unaccustomed attitudes in honour of Shakespeare.

When this urge was first felt is difficult to discover. There are, admittedly, the splendid tributes prefacing the First

Folio; and, still more important, there is the fact, never to be taken for granted, that that volume was published at all. But otherwise there is no sign that, for the first hundred years of his posthumous career, Shakespeare was thought of as much more than a dead dramatist, some of whose rather old-fashioned plays could usefully be adapted to the theatrical fashions of the time. Greater veneration began to be felt in the eighteenth century. In 1709, Nicholas Rowe published the first 'edited' collection of the plays and along with it the first serious attempt at a biography. Others soon tried to improve upon Rowe's editorial labours, and by the end of the first half of the century, Shakespeare may be said to have become established as a writer of classic status.

Gradually the desire arose to do public honour to the memory of the man behind the plays. An early manifestation of this desire was the erection in Westminster Abbey of Scheemaker's statue, dedicated in 1741. Perhaps it was this event that made the inhabitants of Stratford notice that the monument in their church needed repair. In 1746 a strolling player, John Ward, and his company of actors performed in the Town Hall. His are the first recorded performances of Shakespeare in the town; one of them was of *Othello*, Mr Ward 'very genteelly refusing to apply a shilling of the money to his own use', but devoting the proceeds to the repair of the monument.

Stratford was slowly becoming a centre of pilgrimage, and among those who had already paid homage was David Garrick, soon to be acknowledged as the greatest actor of the age. In 1768, the Corporation decided that it would like a statue of Shakespeare to adorn its new Town Hall – the fine building that still stands (Plate 1). It did not, however, feel inclined to pay for one. So it was privately suggested to Garrick that he might care to present 'some statue, bust, or picture' of Shakespeare to the town. More publicly, the

Corporation resolved unanimously that Garrick be made an honorary burgess, and directed that the copy of his freedom of the borough 'should be presented to him in a small neat chest constructed from a mulberry tree planted by Shakespeare himself'. Garrick did more than was asked of him. He suggested, organized, and appeared in the series of ceremonies, held in September 1769, that have come to be known as the Garrick Jubilee. The story of the occasion is well known. Hundreds of visitors filled the town for the three-day festival. It began at dawn with the thunder of cannon, the chiming of bells, and the singing of mummers; there was a ceremony at which Garrick was officially appointed Steward of the Jubilee. Flowers were placed on the grave, and Arne's oratorio *Judith* – dedicated to Garrick – was sung. The visitors wore medals and ribbons designed by Garrick. There was a grand parade, led by Garrick. There were songs written (by Garrick) in praise of Shakespeare – 'Sweet Willy-O' was a favourite. Buildings were decorated with transparencies. There were fireworks galore. Garrick recited to musical accompaniment an ode he had written, and made a superbly histrionic speech. There was a fancy-dress ball, at which the guests included James Boswell as an armed Corsican chief. There was horse-racing. There was a considerable amount of rain. There was indeed so much rain that a pageant of Shakespeare characters that had been carefully prepared had to be cancelled.

One omission from the 1769 celebration has often been deplored: on no occasion was Shakespeare permitted to speak for himself. None of his plays – not even an excerpt from one of them – was performed throughout the festival. Yet the participants seem to have been satisfied. Admittedly, the jubilee had its detractors; one – Samuel Foote, the actor – wrote:

A jubilee, as it hath lately appeared, is a public invitation circulated and arranged by puffing to go posting without horses to an obscure borough without representatives governed by a Mayor and Aldermen who are no magistrates, to celebrate a great poet whose works have made him immortal by an ode without poetry, music without melody, dinners without victuals, and lodging without bed; a masquerade when half the people appear barefaced, a horse race up to the knees in water, fireworks extinguished as soon as they were lighted, and a gingerbread amphitheatre which tumbled to pieces as soon as it was finished.

Admittedly, too, the occasion showed a loss of £2,000. It had been agreed that responsibility for any loss should be shared between the town and Garrick, but the actor generously offered to defray it all himself, and eventually did so. A newspaper reported sarcastically that 'of all involved in the jubilee Garrick was the greatest loser, and the greatest gainer was a Mr M— who made a fortune selling Balsam of Honey to those who caught cold'. But there was consolation for the town, which got both a statue and a picture (Plate 32a), as well as some invaluable publicity; and there was consolation for Garrick, too: he staged the cancelled pageant as part of a satirical play, *The Jubilee*, at Drury Lane, where it had a record run of ninety-one performances.

Although the celebrations at Stratford-upon-Avon were an easy target for the satirist (and such celebrations still are), there were those who respected Garrick's efforts to establish the veneration of Shakespeare in this public form. Among them was the poet William Cowper who complimented Garrick in his poem *The Task*:

> He drew the liturgy, and fram'd the rites
> And solemn ceremonial of the day,
> And call'd the world to worship on the banks
> Of Avon, fam'd in song. Ah, pleasant proof
> That piety has still in human hearts
> Some place, a spark or two not yet extinct!

Minor celebrations continued to be held in succeeding years, but it was not till the early nineteenth century that they came to be associated with 23 April, traditionally the day of Shakespeare's birth and death, as well as St George's Day. The death anniversary was commemorated in a small way in 1816. In 1820, Leigh Hunt wrote his essay 'Shakespeare's Birthday':

The lustre and utility of intellectual power is so increasing in the world, that we do not despair of seeing the time when his birthday will be a subject of public rejoicing; when the regular feast will be served up in tavern and dwelling-house, the bust crowned with laurel, and the theatres sparkle with illuminations.

And Leigh Hunt offered suggestions how the event might be celebrated within the family circle:

If the enthusiasm is in high taste, the ladies should be crowned with violets, which (next to the roses of their lips) seem to have been his [Shakespeare's] favourite flower. After tea should come singing and music, especially the songs which Arne set from his plays, and the ballad of 'Thou soft-flowing Avon'. If an engraving or bust of him could occupy the principal place in the room, it would look like the 'present deity' of the occasion; and we have known a very pleasant effect produced by everybody's bringing some quotation applicable to him from his works, and laying it before his image, to be read in the course of the evening.

In 1824 the Shakespeare Club was founded in Stratford to organize annual birthday celebrations, with a 'jubilee' every third year. But their banquets aroused some indignant protests. Not far from Charlecote lived the descendants of the nearest relative to Shakespeare (his sister Joan), in unnoticed and unmitigated poverty. 'The Shakespeare Club has gone down to Stratford, and feasted and guzzled *in honour of Shakespeare*, and the representatives of Shakespeare in the place have been left in their poverty,' wrote

William Howitt in his famous book *Homes and Haunts of the Most Eminent British Poets* in 1847. Is there the remotest connexion 'between the achievements of pure intellect and the seven-gallon-barrel stomach of anniversary topers? Between the exquisite productions of a divine imagination, and the uproarious riot of a public feed when half-seas over?' 'Is it not a precious imposture,' Howitt wrathfully exclaimed, 'to make a feast to a man's honour, and not to invite to it his nearest relatives, especially when they live at the next door? In the name of the national reputation, let this wretched and egotistic farce be put down by the good sense of the British public! If these people will not honour Shakespeare by honouring his family, let them at least abstain from insulting their poverty and their neglect by this public parade, and this devouring of joints.'

The impoverished members of Shakespeare's kin, whose fate aroused some interest and some compassion in the nineteenth century, were indeed descended from Joan, the poet's sister. She married a certain William Hart, a hatter of Stratford, and died in 1646, leaving only one son (Thomas) surviving her. There were two grandsons of Joan Hart, Thomas and George; and to them the last direct descendant of the poet, his granddaughter Elizabeth (later Lady Barnard), on her death in 1670 bequeathed Shakespeare's house in Henley Street. Of these George, who died in 1702, left issue; and his descendants had the honour of being the representatives of the poet's family and continued to occupy the western part of the house, which they eventually began to show to visitors as Shakespeare's Birthplace. Later in the eighteenth century they fell increasingly into poverty; John Hart (sixth in descent from Joan) moved to Tewkesbury, where he carried on the occupation of chair-mender. His son, William Shakespeare Hart, a turner, who also lived at Tewkesbury, and died in 1834, was accustomed to exhibit a walking-stick which he alleged to have been Shakespeare's. In 1848

Thomas Shakespeare Hart, eighth in descent from Joan, was found to be employed as a rush-chair mender at Tewkesbury. He died in 1850, and his son George, in the 1860s, emigrated to Australia, where there are still descendants of the family. A George Shakespeare Hart of High Wycombe, who died in 1907, was educated at Stratford Grammar School, and had a son named Alfred Thomas Shakespeare Hart. But as well as this main line of the Harts, there were other descendants of Joan, on the female side of the family; several of the daughters had married Smiths. William Howitt, who visited Stratford in the 1830s, and published an account of it in his *Visits to Remarkable Places* (1840), found a boy called William Shakespeare Smith at school there, and prided himself on having picked him out of the class by noticing the 'Shakespeare cast of countenance'. He, too, is reported to have subsequently emigrated to Australia. In the middle of the nineteenth century there was a William Smith of this family keeping a public house at Tewkesbury. These were the worthy folk of Shakespeare's kin – chair-menders and tavern-keepers – who were not invited to participate in the celebrations and banquetings in honour of the immortal Shakespeare.

The festival of 1827 included the opening of the town's first permanent theatre; it stood till 1872. The Birthplace was bought for the nation in 1847. By the time of the third centenary of Shakespeare's birth, 23 April had, largely as a result of the Shakespeare Club's efforts, become firmly established as the date on which celebrations should centre.

The elaboration of the Shakespeare ritual – the national possession of the birthplace and the death place, the popularity of festivals and feasts, the interest in relics and records, together with the gigantic position of Shakespeare in English literature – very naturally led to a scheme for a national memorial. This had for long been discussed. The eighteenth

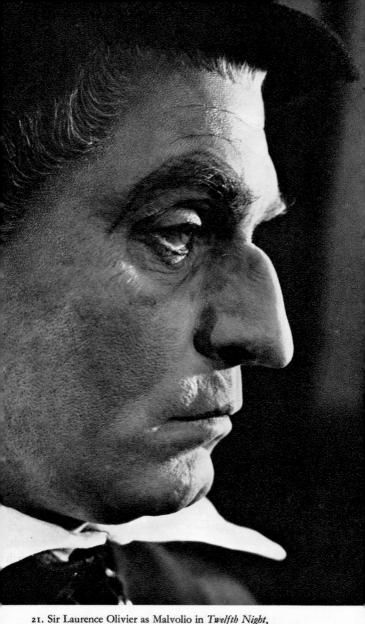

21. Sir Laurence Olivier as Malvolio in *Twelfth Night*,
Stratford-upon-Avon, 1955.

22a. Paul Scofield as King Lear and Alan Webb as Gloucester, Stratford-upon-Avon, 1962.

22b. Sir Laurence Olivier as Richard III, and Sir Ralph Richardson as Richmond, the Old Vic, 1944-5.

23a. A scene from Sir Tyrone Guthrie's production of *All's Well That Ends Well*, Stratford-upon-Avon, 1959.

23b. A scene from the National Youth Theatre's production of *Hamlet*, Sarah Bernhardt Theatre, Paris, 1960.

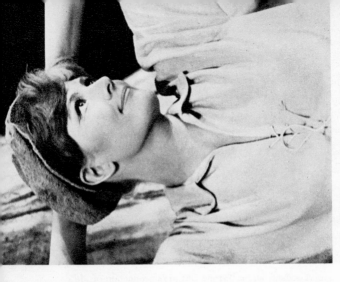

24a. Peter O'Toole as Shylock, Stratford-upon-Avon, 1960.

24b. Vanessa Redgrave as Rosalind in *As You Like It*, Stratford-upon-Avon, 1961.

26a. The interior of the Old Vic Theatre, London.

26b. The Royal Shakespeare Theatre, Stratford-upon-Avon.

27a. The Festival Theatre, Stratford, Ontario, Canada.

27b. A scene from Sir Tyrone Guthrie's production of
Richard III at Stratford, Ontario, 1953, showing Sir Alec Guinness
as Richard.

28a. Asta Nielson as Hamlet in the film, Denmark, 1920.

28b. Douglas Fairbanks and Mary Pickford in the film of
The Taming of the Shrew, 1929.

29a. Sergei Bondarchuk as Othello and Andrei Popov as Iago in the Russian film of *Othello*, 1956.

29b. A scene from Max Reinhardt's film of *A Midsummer Night's Dream*, 1936.

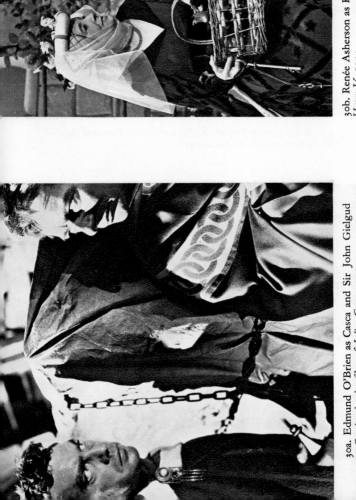

30a. Edmund O'Brien as Casca and Sir John Gielgud as Cassius in the film of *Julius Caesar*, 1952.

30b. Renée Asherson as Katharine in Olivier's film of *Henry V*, 1944.

31b. Sir Laurence Olivier in the film of *Hamlet*, 1948.

31a. Sir Laurence Olivier as Henry V in the film.

32b. The Apotheosis of Garrick, by George Carter, 1784. Members of Garrick's company dressed for Shakespearian roles, wave farewell as Garrick is wafted

32a. David Garrick with a bust of Shakespeare: by Thomas

century at least saw the setting-up of Scheemaker's statue in Poets' Corner in Westminster Abbey by public subscription (1741). Garrick at the time of the Jubilee of 1769 had suggested that a school of acting should be established at Stratford to commemorate the actor-dramatist. Others repeated this proposal or made similar suggestions. But the greater part of the nineteenth century passed with nothing done. Discussions began in 1821, when Walter Scott, Coleridge, Tom Moore, Washington Irving, and other eminent names, showed themselves to be interested. But nothing came of these efforts, and the money was returned to the subscribers. It is remarkable, wrote Douglas Jerrold ironically, that England should, even at the present time, only a little more than two centuries after his death, have already begun to think of the propriety of erecting, at some future day, a national monument to her poet.

As the tercentenary of 1864 drew near the demand for a memorial became more insistent. In June 1863 a National Shakespeare Tercentenary Celebration Committee was formed in London. The principal promoter was William Hepworth Dixon, the editor of the *Athenaeum*. He had visions of a £30,000 monument to Shakespeare. The strongest arguments were forthcoming for thus safeguarding the honour of England. John Heraud, the dramatic critic, eloquently pleaded for a memorial 'as an acknowledgment to Providence for the gift of a man of genius to a nation; as an assurance that such nation in some sort merits such a gift'. The conscience of the people has been awakened, and (continued Heraud ominously) 'it will be no longer safe to defer to an indefinite period the public expression of that thankfulness for Shakespeare which it would be ignominious not to feel. The people will not accept complicity with the powerful and wealthy who have declined to contribute from their ample means to support the scheme for a national memorial. They will demand, for the sake of England, that honour shall be given where honour is due. They will demand it, not by menace or violence, but by the greater force of example. They are about to subscribe their pennies and will thus compel the children of Mammon to subscribe their pounds.'

A committee was formed; a letter was sent to *The Times* announcing the scheme; and various celebrities were invited to become vice-presidents or members of the executive committee, including (as representatives of literature) Bulwer Lytton, Ruskin, Tennyson, Dickens, and Thackeray.

There was, of course, a large number of grandiose plans, improbable of fulfilment. Someone wanted a huge tower to be built, with a brick core but covered with porcelain tiles which made up scenes from Shakespeare's plays. There were schemes for a great avenue (in imitation of the Champs Élysées) from Portland Place to the summit of Primrose Hill, where a monument was to be placed to dominate London, two hundred feet above sea-level. Benjamin Webster issued an appeal to the Shakespeare Committee to devote their money and energies to found, in Shakespeare's name, a home for retired and worn-out actors.

Punch joined the most important part of the literary world in thinking that Shakespeare needed no monument (see opposite page) and that the whole scheme was an object of derision.

What needs my SHAKESPEARE for his honoured bones,
The sov'reigns of BROWN, ROBINSON, and JONES?
Or that his hallowed relics should be hid
Under a HEPWORTH–DIXON pyramid?
Dear son of memory – great heir of fame,
Why all these little names tacked to thy name?
Thou may'st feel wonder and astonishment
At all this row about thy monument,
While to the shame of our dramatic Art,
Thy plays of our stage-banquet make no part.

Shakespeare and the Pigmies: from *Punch*, 1864

In 1864, in fact, celebrations were held far and wide. The centre was, understandably enough, Stratford. Preparations had begun there in 1859, but were not undertaken seriously till 1863. In September of that year Robert Hunter was appointed secretary of the Stratford Committee; he held the office for six months, after which, he says, 'I resigned, and subsequently rapidly recovered my health and spirit'. It is clear from his account of the celebrations, published soon after they were over, that his period of office was riddled with anxiety. His nervousness may be gauged from a quotation on his title page; it is from the *Daily News*, and reads:

It should not be overlooked that the Stratford authorities have undertaken an onerous and costly scheme in deference to the public voice of demand. It is also to be remembered that the matter will be discussed a hundred years hence, with sharp curiosity, to discern what the appreciation of Shakespeare really was about the year 1863.

The story that the secretary tells is long, complicated, and rather sad. There were many troubles. For instance, there was much competition from London, where many people thought that the celebrations would more properly be held. But the Mayor of Stratford felt that 'in these railway times' they should be at Stratford. There was an embarrassing incident over actors: someone unwisely asked the Frenchman, Charles Fechter, to play Hamlet; the leading English actor, Samuel Phelps, was deeply offended, and made no attempt to disguise the fact. Eventually, neither actor appeared, nor was *Hamlet* on the programme. Other performers fell out for one reason or another, and the programme changed continually up to the last minute. The organizers worked hard, but they blundered in various ways. The advertising was bad: the main poster 'was about as useful as an old newspaper on the walls'. The terrible result was that, on the first day of the festival, though the town had been completely refurbished for the occasion and though the weather was splendid, there was, in Hunter's words, 'a degree of ominous quietude throughout the streets which on such an occasion was most remarkable'. The fortnight that followed showed a similar mingling of good and bad fortune. There were some splendid fireworks, but 'the brilliancy of the finale' – an illuminated portrait of Shakespeare – 'was sadly marred by the density of the smoke'. The Punch and Judy show and the menagerie 'had to make a speedy exit as the expected multitude had not arrived in Stratford'; a balloon was to have made an ascent, but, astonishingly, there was not enough gas to inflate it. Once again a pageant gave trouble: this time, because it had not been included on the official list of events. The populace of Stratford has a weakness for such things; it wanted a pageant and, by setting up a special committee, it got one.

There were, however, for the official Committee some compensating factors. The birthday banquet, attended by 750 guests, was a great success. It concluded with toasts to the Queen; the Prince and Princess of Wales; the memory of Shakespeare; the Archbishops and the Bishops and clergy; the Army, Navy, Yeomanry, and Volunteers; the Drama; the Earl of Carlisle; the Poets of England; the Poets of Ireland; the Poets of Scotland; the Poets of America; the Visitors; and the Mayor and Corporation of the Borough of Stratford. During the two weeks, several plays were performed with reasonable success; so was Handel's *Messiah*; and the secretary derived a final melancholic satisfaction from the fact that 'no widow or orphan associates his or her bereavement with this joyful occasion'. The festival had started with higher aims than merely avoiding the slaughter of any of the inhabitants; the organizers had wished to provide scholarships for the grammar-school and a memorial for the town. These plans fell through: the occasion was a

financial failure. But Stratford had done its best for Shakespeare.

Hunter's book compels respect for the townsmen's efforts and sympathy with the weariness expressed in their preliminary announcement, where they wrote: 'After many
months of unceasing exertion, rendered more onerous by
their entire inexperience and by the difficulty of selecting
amongst the vast number of suggestions which have been
offered from all parts of the word, the Committee are now
in a position to announce the general features of their programme.'

The Birthday Sermon was preached by Archbishop
Trench, a man of letters of eminence, and he told his con-
gregation that 'those who mould a nation's life should be
men acquainted with God's scheme of the universe, cheerfully working in their own appointed sphere the work which
has been assigned to them, accepting God's world because it
is His.' Shakespeare was one of these. The next day was
Sunday, and Charles Wordsworth, Bishop of St Andrews,
preached on 'Man's Excellency a Cause of Praise and Thankfulness to God', and he demonstrated, among other interesting things, that the gentle Shakespeare was justified
in using such strong language about filial ingratitude
in *King Lear* by his own dutiful behaviour towards his
parents.

The American participation in the cult of Shakespeare
and contribution to the celebrations were notable. The tercentenary year came in the troubled times of the Civil War
when relations between the United States and England were
strained. But the occasion was honoured by a proposal to
erect a statue in Central Park, New York. The foundation
stone was laid on 23 April 1864 and the statue was dedicated
in 1872, with an address by the poet William Cullen Bryant
and a reading by Edwin Booth. And Bayard Taylor wrote a
dignified ode on the occasion:

Here in his might he stands!
No sweep of earth-dividing seas can bar
The breeze of morning or the morning star
From visiting our lands:
His wit, the breeze, his wisdom, as the star,
Shone where our earliest life was set, and blew
To freshen deed and plan
In brains American . . .
To urge, resist, encourage and subdue!
He came, a household ghost we could not ban:
He sat on winter-nights, by cabin fires;
His summer fairies linked their hands
Along our yellow sands;
He preached within the shadow of our spires:
And when the certain Fate drew nigh to cleave
The birth-chord, and a separate being leave,
He in our ranks of patient-hearted men
Wrought with the boundless forces of his fame,
Victorious, and became
The Master of our Thought, the Land's first Citizen.

Out of the tercentenary activity, and especially out of the success of the performance of plays at Stratford, there eventually emerged a better idea of a Shakespeare memorial, and the scheme was renewed under happier auspices at the loyal native town. The small theatre that had been built in 1827 in the gardens of New Place and had seen many Shakespeare plays at various times was pulled down in 1872 in order to clear the gardens entirely and lay them out tastefully. A temporary theatre had been constructed for the 1864 performances. But in 1874 Charles Edward Flower, a member of a distinguished Stratford family, offered a site and a considerable donation to start a national memorial, consisting of a theatre, picture-gallery, library, and annual celebrations of the birthday with performances of the plays. There was, as usual, some opposition from the men of letters. But the money was collected, and the theatre, designed in an interesting Gothic style by W. F. Unsworth, opened on Shakespeare's birthday in 1879 with a performance of *Much Ado About Nothing*, with Helena Faucit as Beatrice (it was her last appearance) and Barry Sullivan as Benedick. The Memorial Theatre at Stratford was one of the boldest actions in honour of Shakespeare during the Victorian age. It was deservedly successful, and (as the whole world knows) it has been lasting. Only a few parts of the original buildings survived the fire of 1926.

Meanwhile, statues of Shakespeare, as tokens of the national cult, had begun to spring up. Hitherto the only important ones (apart from the bust in Holy Trinity Church, Stratford) had been the one in Westminster Abbey and those arranged by Garrick for his Stratford Jubilee. In 1874 Albert Grant (later Baron Grant) gave the statue in Leicester Square, London, made by Fontana; but it is little more than a copy of the one in Westminster Abbey. Private memorials began to appear in Stratford and elsewhere. An American newspaper proprietor named George William Childs was particularly interested in spending his money on memorials to literary men. In honour of Shakespeare he bestowed a drinking fountain on the Rother Market in 1887, designed by J. A. Cossins and decorated it with the temperance motto:

Honest water, which ne'er left man i' the mire
(*Timon of Athens*)

and with a delicate compliment to Queen Victoria – it was the year of her Golden Jubilee:

In her days every man shall eat in safety
Under his own vine what he plants; and sing
The merry songs of peace to all his neighbours.
God shall be truly known; and those about her
From her shall read the perfect ways of honour,
And by those claim their greatness – not by blood.
(*Henry VIII*)

The fountain was unveiled by Henry Irving, who read a poem by Oliver Wendell Holmes especially written for the occasion.

The following year (1888) a more remarkable memorial appeared in Stratford. An amateur sculptor, Lord Ronald Sutherland Gower, designed and executed in Paris a monument consisting of the poet sitting in meditation with an expression of great intensity; below are four of his principal characters: Hamlet, Henry V, Lady Macbeth, and Falstaff. It was presented to Stratford-upon-Avon by its creator and set up in the gardens of the theatre (but it was later moved to its present site near Clopton Bridge). The inscriptions are less moral and more poetical than those on the Childs monument: 'Good night, sweet prince, and flights of angels sing thee to thy rest'; 'Life's but a walking shadow, a poor player that struts and frets his hour upon the stage'; and so on.

Shakespeare's associates, too, were not forgotten, even when it was not possible to erect authentic statues of *them*. John Heminges and Henry Condell had been buried in St Mary Aldermanbury, London, the parish in which they had lived for many years. In 1896 in their honour a statue of Shakespeare on a pedestal was placed there, including a representation of the title page of the First Folio, which they had given to the world 'only to keep the memory of so worthy a friend and fellow alive as was our Shakespeare'.

Most of these effigies made an effort to represent Shakespeare with a portraiture which fulfilled legitimate expectation of intelligence and imagination in England's great poet. It was a common (but by no means universal) opinion that neither the Stratford monument (Plate 9a) nor the Droeshout engraving (Plate 14) give adequate representations of the wisdom and sensibility that must have shone out from Shakespeare's face. Ideal portraits (as well as deliberate forgeries) have appeared from the eighteenth century onwards. Gainsborough's bust in his portrait of Garrick (Plate 32a) is of some beauty. But none of the unauthentic portraits has succeeded in ousting the image provided by the Droeshout engraving, which has disseminated the Shakespeare features throughout the world on innumerable objects; pots and trays, napkins and table-cloths, trade-marks and inn-signs If one excludes living politicians from consideration, is not the face of Shakespeare the best-known one in the world?

A touching story of an effigy of Shakespeare is told by Thackeray in his *Memorials of Gormandizing*—the discovery of a remarkable portrait in Paris. An English gentleman who collected paintings was told by a Parisian lady that she had in her possession one of the greatest rarities in the world – a picture admirable, too, as a work of art – no less than an original portrait of Shakespeare, by his comrade, the famous John Davis. The Englishman rushed off immediately to behold the wonder, and saw a head, rudely but vigorously painted on a panel, about twice the size of life, with a couple of hooks drawn through the top part of the board, under which was written:

THE WILLIAM SHAKESPEARE

BY JOHN DAVIS

'*Voyez-vous, Monsieur,*' said the lady, '*il n'y a plus de doute. Le portrait de Shakespeare, du célèbre Davis, et signé même de lui!*' 'I remember,' continued Thackeray, 'it used to hang up in a silent little street in the Latin quarter, near an old convent, before a quaint old quiet tavern that I loved. It was pleasant to see the old name written up in a strange land, and the well-known friendly face greeting one. There was a quiet little garden at the back of the tavern, and famous good roast beef, clean rooms, and English beer'.

National plans to commemorate the tercentenary of Shakespeare's death were discussed as early as 1904, and became associated with the movement to establish a National Theatre. The War made it necessary to reduce the proposed scale of events in 1916; but the occasion was marked by a number of ceremonies and special publications, including *A Book of Homage to Shakespeare*, which emphasized the international interest in Shakespeare. Nowadays the celebrations on 23 April each year are attended by delegates from a large and ever increasing number of countries. Ambassadors, ministers, and diplomatic representatives, from states great and small, old and new, assemble and walk in the procession from the Birthplace to the grave in Holy Trinity Church. The success of the Royal Shakespeare Theatre Company in the building (Plate 26b) opened on the birthday in 1932 has contributed to the increasing international reputation of Shakespeare by its performances in many parts of the world, and the activities of the Shakespeare Birthplace Trust have made the town of Stratford-upon-Avon a worthy and worthwhile centre for the celebration of Shakespeare.

The fourth centenary of the birthday is being honoured with unparalleled activity. New biographies, critical studies, and other tributes are being published. At Covent Garden we see operas based on plays by Shakespeare; the occasion is being celebrated on radio and television; and professional and amateur theatre groups all over England are presenting special performances. Lectures are delivered, banquets consumed, toasts drunk, and speeches made in Shakespeare's honour. There are special postage stamps, and commemorative objects abound. The celebrations are confined neither to England nor to English-speaking countries. But once again, as in 1769 and 1864, the centre of celebrations is Stratford-upon-Avon. In the town of Shakespeare's birth, the Royal Shakespeare Company is performing the great cycle of his plays on English history. The new Shakespeare Centre, planned by the Birthplace Trust, and opened as a royal occasion, brings together rich collections of books and archives. An ambitious Exhibition, also to be seen in Edinburgh and London, makes vivid the life and times of Shakespeare. Musical programmes include newly commissioned settings of words by Shakespeare. Never before, probably, will so much have been done in honour of one man: an actor, poet, and playwright, born four hundred years ago. And the climax comes on 23 April when the representatives of many nations, having walked through the Birthplace and along the streets of Stratford, past New Place, the Guild Chapel, and the grammar-school, lay flowers on the grave in Holy Trinity Church where lie, still undisturbed, the remains of William Shakespeare.

NOTES ON
THE CONTRIBUTORS

JOHN RUSSELL BROWN, senior lecturer in English, the University
of Birmingham. Author of *Shakespeare and his Comedies*. Editor of
The Merchant of Venice (New Arden Shakespeare) and John
Webster's *The White Devil* and *The Duchess of Malfi* (Revels
Plays). Joint Editor of *Stratford-upon-Avon Studies* and *The
Stratford-upon-Avon Library*.

LAURENCE KITCHIN is the author of *Mid-Century Drama*
(Faber), an influential survey of new writing and classical acting. He
represents the United Kingdom on the editorial committee of *World
Theatre*. Broadcasts on 'The Critics' and frequently on the Third
Programme.

KENNETH MUIR, Professor of English Literature, the University
of Liverpool. Author of *The Voyage to Illyria*; *Shakespeare as
Collaborator*; *Last Periods (Shakespeare, Racine, Ibsen)*; *Shakespeare's
Sources*; *Shakespeare: the Great Tragedies*; *Shakespeare and the
Tragic Pattern*; *John Milton*; *The Life and Letters of Sir Thomas
Wyatt*. Editor of *Macbeth* and *King Lear* (New Arden Shakespeare);
Elizabethan Lyrics; *The Collected Poems of Sir Thomas Wyatt*;
Unpublished Poems of Sir Thomas Wyatt; *The Pelican Book of
English Prose, I*. Translator of *Five Plays of Racine*.

NORMAN SCARFE, lecturer in History, the University of Leicester. Author of *Suffolk, a Shell Guide*; *Letters from the Peninsula,
The Freer Family Correspondence 1807–14*; *Clare Priory, the Story
of a Suffolk House*.

CHARLES J. SISSON, Professor Emeritus of English Language and
Literature, the University of London. Author of *Le goût publique et
le théâtre élisabéthain*; *Thomas Lodge and other Elizabethans*; *Lost*

Plays of Shakespeare's Age; *The Judicious Marriage of Mr Hooker*; *The Mythical Sorrows of Shakespeare*; *New Readings in Shakespeare.* Editor of *William Shakespeare, the Complete Works.*

T. J. B. SPENCER, Professor of English Language and Literature and Director of the Shakespeare Institute, the University of Birmingham. Author of *Fair Greece, Sad Relic: Literary Philhellenism from Shakespeare to Byron*; *The Tyranny of Shakespeare*; *Byron and the Greek Tradition*; *From Gibbon to Darwin.* Editor of *Shakespeare's Plutarch* (Peregrine Books). General Editor of *The Modern Language Review.*

JOHN RUSSELL TAYLOR, Film Critic of *The Times*, has written widely on theatre, films, and television. Books include *Anger and After: A Guide to the New British Drama* (Penguin) and *Anatomy of a Television Play.*

STANLEY WELLS, Fellow of the Shakespeare Institute, the University of Birmingham. Contributor to *Shakespeare Survey*, *Shakespeare Quarterly*, *Theatre Notebook*, and other periodicals.

*Some other books published by Penguins
are described on the following pages*

THE LIFE OF SHAKESPEARE

F. E. Halliday

On 26 April 1564 'Gulielmus filius Johannes Shakspere' was christened at Holy Trinity Church at Stratford-upon-Avon, and on 25 April 1616 'Will Shakspere, gent' was buried at the same church. In between lived the man we know as William Shakespeare.

Modern scholarship has enormously enriched our understanding of Shakespeare's plays and of the world in which he moved and wrote, yet it is now ten years since the last full-scale biography of Shakespeare was written. Mr Halliday, using recent research – in particular the work of Leslie Hotson and T. W. Baldwin – steers a lively course between the meagre dust of contemporary records and the higher fancies of Shakespeare's 'lost years'.

'A quick-moving and workmanlike biography ... admirably compact and comprehensive . . . we are given as much information as others have provided in twice the length' – Ivor Brown in the *Observer*

'He is thorough, he is wary, and he is hardly ever over-pedantic' – Alan Dent in the *Sunday Telegraph*

THE AGE OF SHAKESPEARE

Edited by Boris Ford

This volume covers the period of Shakespeare's own lifetime. It contains a long general survey of the English literary renaissance, and also an account of the social context of literature in the period. Then there follow a number of essays which consider in detail the work and importance of individual dramatists and poets and prose-writers, but above all the dramatists, for this was their age: five of the essays are devoted to Shakespeare's plays alone. Finally, this volume contains an appendix giving short author-biographies and, in each case, standard editions of authors' works, critical commentaries, and lists of books for further study and reference.

One of the volumes of the Pelican Guide to English Literature

LIFE IN SHAKESPEARE'S ENGLAND

John Dover Wilson

Many people who have learned to enjoy Shakespeare feel they would like to know more about his life and times, and this authoritative book, reprinted again in Pelicans, is the answer. It is not a biographical study, but an anthology collected from many contemporary sources so as to illuminate the conditions, the appearance, the habits, pastimes, and beliefs of Shakespeare's time. Professor Dover Wilson's method of assembling this panorama of the period is to pin-point the clues provided by scores of passages in the plays and follow them up by relevant supporting evidence from what we nowadays call the 'documentary' writers of the time. Thus we are able to see city and countryside, school and university, court and theatre, as the man of Shakespeare's day saw them with his own eyes. We observe at close quarters his sports, his superstitions, his daily life at home or abroad, his experiences in childhood and age. Actor, sailor, courtier, traveller, and beggar relate, in their own words, what living was like in the great days of sixteenth-century England.

A SHORT HISTORY OF ENGLISH LITERATURE

Sir Ifor Evans

The first edition of Sir Ifor Evans's *Short History of English Literature* was acclaimed by Ivor Brown in the *Observer* as follows:

'Professor Evans writes to the classical model, as brief, as lucid. He relates the arts to society instead of penning them in the study. As a judge he is tolerant and undogmatic, but never slack in his standards. He is fair to all and gushes over none. . . . This justice of approach is coupled with a mastery of phrase which makes the writing lively without being exhaustingly exhibitionist in judgement or epigrammatic in style.'

Since its first appearance it has served countless readers as an invaluable map to the broad field of English literature. Now, revised throughout, and extended to include the major poets, dramatists, and novelists of the post-war period, it is with us again, as reliable and readable a guide as ever, but with wider range and a more recent perspective.

THE GROWTH AND STRUCTURE OF ELIZABETHAN COMEDY

M. C. Bradbrook

Her published works on Elizabethan drama are evidence that Miss Bradbrook is uniquely qualified to carry out a full-scale survey of the comedy of the period, to which so little attention has been given. As she states in her introduction to this book: 'Comedies outnumber tragedies on the Elizabethan stage by nearly three to one. Sweet and bitter comedy, romantic and satiric comedy, or Shakespearian and Jonsonian comedy have all been used as terms of description for the two main divisions, of which the first may be said to be characteristically Elizabethan, and the second Jacobean. In the following chapters I have tried to trace the evolution and the interaction of these two comic forms.'

In this scholarly study she follows the course of English comedy from its beginnings, commenting on the plays of Shakespeare, Jonson, Lyly, Peele, Greene, Nashe, Dekker, Marston, Middleton, Day, Chapman, and Fletcher. In addition she discusses the significant period of the War of the Theatres (1599–1602).

'The criticism of individual playwrights is fresh and penetrating, and at times Miss Bradbrook's writing has the compression and force of epigram' – *Listener*

'An invaluable guide to the whole corpus of "sweet and bitter comedy" from Lyly to Fletcher' – J. I. M. Stewart in the *New Statesman*

A SHAKESPEARE COMPANION

F. E. Halliday

'Nothing quite like this has been done before ... the comprehensiveness, clarity, and reliability of the work as a whole are positive virtues which will make it extremely valuable to all students of Shakespeare' - *The Times Educational Supplement*

This volume provides a simple and handy index to all aspects of Shakespearian lore over three and a half centuries. As the author himself explains, 'It is a handbook not only to Shakespeare's life and works, but also to friends and acquaintances, to his poems and plays and their characters, but also to the Elizabethan–Jacobean theatre, the other dramatists who wrote for it, their most important plays and the companies that performed them, and to the history up to the present day of Shakespeare's work both on the stage and in the study, to his printers and publishers, players and producers, editors and adapters, scholars and critics.'

'Everyone from sceptical schoolboys to devotees grown old in Shakespearian wisdom, will find a *livre de chevet* in Mr Halliday's "Companion" ' - *Sunday Times*

SHAKESPEARE'S TRAGEDIES

AN ANTHOLOGY OF MODERN CRITICISM

Edited by Laurence D. Lerner

Shakespeare's tragedies have always been fertile acres for comment and criticism. The same dramas which inspired a Keats to
write poetry appealed to A. C. Bradley - or to Ernest Jones, the
psycho-analyst - as studies of character; and where the New
Criticism has been principally interested in language and
imagery, other critics in America have seen the plays as superb
examples of plot and structure. Most of Aristotle's elements of
tragedy have found their backers, and - as the editor points out
in his introduction - these varying approaches to Shakespeare
are by no means incompatible.

In this volume Laurence Lerner has assembled the best
examples of the modern schools of criticism and arranged them
according to the plays they deal with. With its 'Suggestions for
Further Reading' and the general sections on tragedy, this is a
book which will stimulate the serious reader and do much to
illuminate Shakespearian drama.

SHAKESPEARE'S PLUTARCH

Also edited by T. J. B. Spencer

'Worthy to stand with Malory's *Morte D'Arthur* on either side the English Bible' – George Wyndham on North's Plutarch (1895)

Shakespeare's use of his sources has always been of absorbing interest, and North's translation of Plutarch's *Parallel Lives* of Greek and Roman heroes is among the most important of these. In this volume an important editorial task has been undertaken by Professor T. J. B. Spencer, Director of the Shakespeare Institute and Professor of English at Birmingham University. Four lives from North's Plutarch – those of Julius Caesar, Brutus, Marcus Antonius, and Coriolanus – have been collated with extracts from the plays for which they were the main sources. In this way the reader can see, almost at a glance, how and why Shakespeare adapted his source.

These colourful biographies must have been a rich reading experience in an age when books were scarce. Plutarch's understanding of character and North's refreshingly vigorous use of the young English language ensure that they are still a joy to read in themselves. And for anyone who has sensed the creative vitality of the great plays, this volume offers a new and exciting opportunity to explore their workmanship.

1736†